DR. JAM

RACISM
and the CHURCH

RACISM and the CHURCH

Printed in the USA.

Cover Design & Layout by Wendy K. Walters

www.wendykwalters.com

Prepared for Publication by: Palm Tree Productions

www.palmtreeproductions.com

ISBN (Print): 978-0-9908749-1-1
ISBN (Kindle): 978-0-9908749-0-4
ISBN (eBook): 978-0-9908749-2-8
Library of Congress Control Number: 2014952862

Scripture translations and other reference materials are listed in the endnotes following each chapter.

TO CONTACT THE AUTHOR:

email: drjamesecollinsministries@ehconline.org

DEDICATION

To my beautiful wife, Brenda, of nearly 33 years, the love
of my life. Without you this would be half a dream.
Also to my wonderful daughters, Jessica and Shawna.
Thank you for your encouragement and patience. It is because
of you that this urgent message has been released from my
heart in obedience to the assignment God has given me.

Jessica, thank you for laboring with me when this work first came
into existence as my thesis in fulfilling my doctoral pursuit.

Thanks to the Deacon Board of Eagle Heights Church
for your full and loving support in this project.

Thanks to Eagle Heights Church for seeking to live
out the heart and the message of this book.

Thanks to Dr. Robert Watkins for our genuine
relationship through which God provided the initial
door of opportunity to fulfill this dream and vision.

Most importantly thanks to Father God who would allow
me the privilege of sharing this urgent message.

There is no one more qualified to tackle the polarizing subject of racism than Dr. James E. Collins. *Racism and the Church* is a must read for all who are leading God's people toward unity. Dr. Collins helps us understand ourselves better and live fruitful lives. I recommend this book to people of all colors and religions—for generations to come."

—DR. ROBERT WATKINS
Kings & Priests Unlimited, Inc.
www.kings-priests.org

Racism and the Church is a powerful call to action for the church. For too long we have pretended racism is no longer an issue in America, and looked to our government or the civil rights movement to solve a problem rooted in sin. Dr. James E. Collins confronts this issue head on—forsaking political correctness and embracing the Word of God as the standard for letting love conquer hate, forgiveness conquer history, and truth conquer lies.

—WENDY K. WALTERS
Author of *Marketing Your Mind* and *Intentionality*
www.wendykwalters.com

CONTENTS

WHOEVER SAYS HE IS IN THE LIGHT AND HATES HIS BROTHER IS STILL IN DARKNESS.

—1 JOHN 2:9 (ESV)

CHAPTER ONE

THE ISSUE OF RACISM

MORE THAN A BLACK AND WHITE ISSUE

Racism is more than a black and white issue. It is a people issue. I can think of no other case that supports this reality more than the following history lesson.

He was born in Austria on April 20, 1889. No one could have known how this little boy would grow up to become a man that would be unbelievably "anointed" by Satan to carry out his diabolical scheme of racism. He was smart, but he was lazy, so he never graduated from high school. Yet, this demented man would rise to great military and political power. In 1919, Adolf Hitler began his campaign of power that was driven by implausible hatred for the Jewish people. He so despised the Jewish people with venom of hatred and disdain that he launched an assault of demonic proportions in 1933 that resulted in the torture and murder of six million Jews. Men, women, children ... not even babies were spared. Sadly, even some church leaders joined the movement speaking out against the Jews. Hitler determined that they must be exterminated, for in his mind they were, "The personification of the devil … the symbol of all evil."[1] Like so many have done, he manipulated biblical scripture and mixed it with religious jargon in an attempt to justify his evil deeds, declaring that by defending himself against the Jews, he was doing the work of the Lord. It was his perverted belief that the Germans were the "master race," superior to all other groups, superior to blacks, gypsies, Poles, Jehovah's Witnesses, homosexuals, and especially the Jews that drove his demonic agenda.

While there are still some who would argue that this never happened, there is plenty of evidence to support the horrible atrocity that became known as the holocaust. It shows just how dangerous racism can be. With this reminder of history I submit that racism is not just a black-white issue, it is in fact a people issue.

Even beyond that, it is not just a people issue. It is an issue among Christians. Several years ago I received phone calls from a number of pastors asking if I would serve on a committee for racial reconciliation. This request came from a group of predominantly white peers. Their own words to me were, "We have begun to realize that there are some prejudices in our own hearts that we must deal with. We are concerned why so many young black pastors are leaving the Assemblies of God. We want to try and change the direction of not only our hearts and the Assemblies of God, but the Body of Christ as a whole."

I was amazed too when I learned that one of the ministers who called me with the invitation to serve was a church planter sent up from the south up to Massachusetts to do just that, plant churches. When he went back to report to his overseers how things were going, he began to tell them about the committee on racial reconciliation that he was helping to start. I was equally amazed, disturbed and heartbroken when he shared their responses with me. He said that he was instructed not to talk about that. They told him, "Down here, we're not prejudiced. But we didn't send you up there for that." They allegedly went on to inform him that continuing down such a road would lead to a loss of financial support should word get around. So we see it is not just an issue with society or an issue for sinners. It is an issue that affects the believer and the non-believer alike.

We also see that this is an issue that is still alive and well in the twenty-first century. On another recent occasion, a friend of mine shared his experience with racism within the walls of the church. His ministry takes him into churches and schools in his southern home state. He told of how he experienced such anger from Christians when President Obama was voted into office. These were churches that were ministering to minorities in the inner cities of the south. In their minds, they were "like Jesus" because they were helping the less fortunate, the poor little black and Mexican children. Yet they could not tolerate or accept the reality that a minority, and in particular a black man, was leading their nation.

RACISM DEFINED

Let me make some very important observations that are rarely addressed in the church when speaking of this tender subject of racism. It must be understood that being prejudiced and being racist are not simultaneously connected. You can be prejudiced without being racist, but, you cannot be racist without being prejudiced. So let's define each word separately, because many times they are associated to circumstance where they are neither appropriate nor accurate.

Prejudice is defined as: 1) a. An adverse judgment or opinion formed beforehand or without knowledge or examination of the facts. b. A preconceived preference or idea or bias. 2) The act or state of holding unreasonable preconceived judgments or convictions.[2] What those definitions state is that one can have a preference or a greater like or dislike for something or someone based on a lack of information. That in itself does not make a person a racist. At some time we all have formed opinions or jumped to conclusions about someone because of their appearance without having all the facts.

For example, when I was growing up, I had white friends whose parents would not invite me over for dinner because they believed that a black child would not like the food they ate. They told their children that it would offend me to have to eat "white people's food." Well, they weren't acting in racism, but in a prejudiced mindset birthed out of ignorance. However, when left unchecked, prejudiced ideas can in turn birth racist attitudes.

LEFT UNCHECKED, PREJUDICED IDEAS BIRTH RACIST ATTITUDES.

As we examine further into the definition, we also find that prejudice can also be an: 3) Irrational suspicion or hatred of a particular group, race or religion.[3] What that tells us is that there is an extreme prejudice that can develop into a racist mentality. In order to define racism there must be a greater definition applied to our understanding of what extreme prejudice looks like. Extreme prejudice is defined as, "irrational dislike or an unfounded hatred, fear or mistrust of a person or group, especially one of a particular religion, ethnicity, nationality, or social status. The notion that one's ethnic stock is superior."[4]

When one reads those definitions, they are very broad, but they serve to help us understand the reality that you can be prejudiced at some level without being racist. But, you cannot be racist without being extremely prejudiced. I state that because I want to make it clear that not everyone who has certain prejudices is a racist, but every racist has a deep-seeded prejudice. The person who is prejudice as defined by the first definition is simply one who is more than likely operating in ignorance.[5] The latter may very well be operating in some ignorance as well, but theirs is dangerous because it is in that area of irrational dislike or an unfound hatred, fear and mistrust of someone simply because they are not "like" them. It is the notion that one's ethnicity makes them superior. It is the belief that human beings are defined by the color of their skin and that different races have different qualities and abilities which cause them to be either inherently superior or inferior to other human beings.

When we consider these definitions we come then to understand that racism is not just a black man/white man issue, it is a people issue. In America there has been so much emphasis on the black/white issue because it has been the racist issue with the greatest potency and human and societal consequence. But we must not confine our thoughts to be read in black and white, for if we do we will undoubtedly miss the reality that Satan uses racism to divide the Body of Christ even in the subtle ways that most do not even realize exist. The church is therefore responsible for acknowledging the obvious and the obscure alike, uprooting racism at its core. Racism that is tolerated anywhere—no matter what form it takes—is racism that is tolerated everywhere. No act stands alone! What touches one will eventually touch us all.

Dr. King addressed this issue while sitting in a prison cell after being arrested in Birmingham, Alabama. While imprisoned he learned of a group of clergy men who were upset about him being in Birmingham. They felt his efforts to help them deal with their racial issues were out of line. On April 12, 1963, after hearing their concerns he wrote a powerful letter of response:

"But more basically, I am in Birmingham because injustice is here. Just as the eighteenth century prophets left their villages and carried their 'Thus saith the Lord' far beyond the boundaries of their home towns, and just as the Apostle Paul left his little village of Tarsus and carried the gospel of Jesus Christ to the far corners of the Greco-Roman world, so am I compelled to carry the gospel of freedom beyond my hometown. Like Paul, I must constantly respond to the Macedonian call for aid. Moreover, I am cognizant of the inter-relatedness of all communities and states. I cannot sit idly by in Atlanta and not be concerned about what happens in Birmingham. Injustice anywhere is a threat to justice everywhere. We are caught in an inescapable network of mutuality, tied in a single garment of destiny. Whatever affects one directly, affects all indirectly. Never again can we afford to live with the narrow provincial 'outside agitator' idea. Anyone who lives inside the United States can never be considered an outsider anywhere it's bounds."[6]

What he was telling us is that we must not have the attitude that says as long as it doesn't touch me personally, it's not about me.

The church in America has not wanted to face this issue head on. Somehow, collectively the body of Christ has assumed the position that if we blow it off, sweep it under the rug and just don't talk about it, it won't affect our group. And in America we found out and continue to see that this is mythological thinking.

RACISM IS A PEOPLE ISSUE

I live in a part of the country, Boston, Massachusetts, where terrorism took a front seat on September 11, 2001. That day, evil men took over airplanes and used them like missiles, seeking to hurt and terrify America in a way like never before. On that dark day, I didn't lose any family; I didn't lose any church members, but I was still affected. On a recent family trip to New York City, I stood at Ground Zero. What I saw twelve years later is that September 11, 2001 still has a stronghold, an effect on this nation. Though not directly affected by this tragedy, those events had an indirect effect on my life, my future, my safety, my perspective. While standing over the memorial, something rose up in me that said I have a responsibility to my country. I have to do my part to make sure this never happens in our nation again. Because what happened to others, happened to me. And as long as racism exists, the church has a responsibility to lift her voice against this evil that is as old as the fall of man. The church needs to understand that what happens to another in the Body of Christ happens to us all.

One thing I have learned, we cannot deal successfully with an issue until we deal with that which is at the root of the issue. In light of the Trayvon Martin murder, Charisma Magazine carried an article, "The Churches Response to Racism," stating, "Racism tarnishes the soul of America."[7] I want to suggest that it is the church's responsibility to war against the spirit of racism with the same assault that we attack other issues that go against the Word of God. The soul of the Body of Christ is tarnished to a degree by our failure to take a stand against racism in the Body of Christ. We must not only address the issue, we must address it with the realization that it is not just a black/white issue. Racism is a people issue. Until we see it as such, we will never see how the stronghold of racism hinders the church from fulfilling the work of the Kingdom.

E N D N O T E S

1. Adler, David A. *We Remember the Holocaust.* New York, New York: Scholastic, Inc., 1989.
2. *The American Heritage Dictionary.* Second Edition. Boston, Massachusetts: Houghton Mifflin Company, 1982, 1985. Print.
3. Ibid.
4. *Microsoft Encarta College Dictionary.* New York, New York: Bloombury Publishing Plc, 2001.
5. *The American Heritage Dictionary.* Second Edition. Boston, Massachusetts: Houghton Mifflin Company, 1982, 1985. Print.
6. Edited by Carson, Clayborne. *The Autobiography of Martin Luther King, Jr.* New York, New York: Grand Central Publishing, 1980.
7. Stang, Steve; Jackson, Harry R., Jr.; Rodriquez, Samuel. "The Churches Response to Racism." Charisma June 2012: 25-30. Print.

CHAPTER TWO

ROOTS OF RACISM

I once heard the story of a man who was on death row for murder. The lawyers defending him held what I believe to be one of the nuttiest defenses I have ever heard. Their defense was the man could not help becoming a murderer because his grandfather was a murderer and his father was a murderer; therefore, he had inherited the murdering gene. I searched but could not find any evidence to back up this defense. Yet, there are people who honestly believe that when we are born, we inherently know the characteristic differences between our own race and those of another race. Some argue that when a baby looks at someone of a different race, they instinctively know they are of a different race. So some are born or have a natural bent toward being racist against other races. But the truth is no one is born a racist. No one comes out of their mother's womb with a "racist gene."

With any issue, and racism is an issue, there can be found a root cause. When I speak of the roots of racism, I am speaking mostly to the prevalent issues that give rise and birth to a racist spirit. I call it a spirit because I believe that ultimately, it is demonically driven by the power of Satan. It is most important that we understand racism is neither a political nor a physical issue, it is a spiritual issue.

RACISM CAN BE ROOTED IN FALSE TEACHING

When I speak of false teaching, I am speaking both of teaching done in Christian churches as well as other religious and cultish environments. In many cases, the Bible is manipulated and used as a tool to back up the false teaching. Please follow along as I share some examples of such teachings. Genesis 9:18-27 says:

> "Now the sons of Noah who went out of the ark were Shem, Ham and Japheth. And Ham was the father of Canaan. These three were the sons of Noah and from these the whole world was populated. Noah began to be a farmer, and he planted a vineyard. Then he drank of the wine and was drunk, and became uncovered in his tent. And Ham, the father of Canaan, saw the nakedness of his father, and told his two brothers outside. But Shem and Japheth took a garment, laid it on both their shoulders, and went in backward and covered the nakedness of their father. Their faces were turned away, and they did not see their father's nakedness. So Noah awoke from his wine, and knew what his younger son had done to him. Then he said, 'Cursed be Canaan; a servant of servants he shall be to his brethren.' And he said, 'Blessed be the Lord, the God of Shem, and may Canaan be his servant. May God enlarge Japheth, and may he dwell in the tents of Shem. And may Canaan be his servant.'"[1]

I heard Pastor Joseph Prince share that in the Jewish community naming their children is a very serious decision. For when they name their child, that name is selected with their destiny—their attributes and their future in mind. In the passage we just read, one of Noah's sons was named Ham, meaning, "black." Noah gets drunk on his own wine. He falls asleep naked. He has no one to cover him. His son Ham discovers him in this embarrassing state. When Ham sees his father's nakedness, instead of doing the righteous thing and covering his father up, he runs out of the tent, goes to his brother's and begins to gossip about it. He runs out yelling at the top of his lungs. He couldn't wait to expose his father's sin. But, Shem and Japheth take a blanket and refuse to look upon their father's nakedness. They walk backward into Noah's tent and place the covering over his naked body. I do not know if they told Noah what had transpired, but when Noah found out what Ham had done, he cursed him.

There are both direct and indirect issues of importance that are present in this encounter that can teach us two different lessons. Let's look at the lesson that is indirectly related to this study. First, this story of Noah and his sons, through a natural relationship, is symbolic of the relationship between spiritual sons and spiritual fathers. I believe there are many in the ministry today who are the stewards of ministries that are blessed because they handled the stumbling of a spiritual leader with integrity, discretion and sensitivity. They did not run out and tell the world when their father's foot slipped. Instead they went into their prayer closet and covered them with prayer. They didn't cover up the sin, but they covered the man. They did what it took to see that their spiritual covering was covered himself. There are others who are witnessing terrible struggle and battles because they responded in the opposite way. I am quite certain that there are those also living under a curse in the ministry today, for when their spiritual father's foot slipped; they could not wait to expose his nakedness. What I am sharing is a biblical truth that seems to be lost in the church today. This is evidenced in the following scriptures:

Galatians 6:8, *"As a man soweth, that shall he reap."*[2]

Matthew 7:2, *"For with what judgment you judge, you will be judged; and with the same measure you use, it will be measured back to you."*[3]

That is the first and equally important lesson that we learn from this encounter.

The second is this: the same scriptures that can be used to justify that truth can be used to justify and perpetuate a lie. When Noah cursed Ham, he cursed him with the curse of slavery. He spoke over his life that his son, Canaan, would become a slave to Japheth and Shem. The curse that he put on him was to run down from Ham's children's generation to his children's children. What I have found is that while scripture may be true, while what is quoted from the Bible may be accurate, it does not mean that every person is accurate in their interpretation. Down through the years there have been theologians who have interpreted this scripture to mean that black people are the descendants of Ham because he was black. The nation of Canaan was cursed. Canaan being the son of Ham was in turn black, therefore supporting the theory that all black people are cursed. This scripture was used powerfully and effectively during the years of slavery in the United States to justify its evil existence. As depicted in the statements in the introduction, blacks were often treated worse than animals. This scripture was used to excuse this treatment by proclaiming the Bible declared blacks as cursed, and who can argue if it is in the Bible?

But let's look at how ridiculous this belief system is. Elretta Dodds makes a powerful argument in the book, *The Trouble with Farrakhan and the Nation of Islam.*

> "Believing this position would be the same as saying that if Ham had big feet, and Canaan had big feet, and Canaan was cursed, then all the people in the world with big feet would be cursed. That's an illogical conclusion of what has been deemed to be the biblical curse."[4]

I agree with her statement because the problem with the "Ham was black and the father of black people, therefore black people are cursed" teaching is that not everyone who has dark skin is black, nor does everyone who is black have dark skin. On one hand I have a friend who is Italian, Sicilian to be exact. His skin is darker than many of my relatives. On the other hand many of these relatives, all of whom are black, are as fair skinned as the average white American. As far back as my family tree is known, there is no recollection or evidence of any white relatives to be found. So, if these biblical scholars are correct in their theory, based on skin color alone, then my Italian friend who is considered white is cursed and my relative who is considered black is not.

Now, there is also a biblical reason why I say their theory is not theologically sound. Galatians 3:13 says, "Christ hath redeemed us from the curse of the law, having become a curse for us; for it is written, cursed is everyone that hangs on a tree …"[5]

The word "curse" is interesting in that it is from the Greek word *"katara"* meaning "curse proceeding from God, the rejection and surrender to punishment, the destruction caused by judgment, the manifested curse." We understand that undoubtedly, Noah had the authority from God to pronounce such a curse on his son. Now, if Christ has indeed redeemed us from the curse of the law, then we are no longer under the law, but under grace. Even if the theologians were correct in their interpretation of the account concerning Ham, what happened then occurred before Christ died to redeem us. Therefore, every curse before, or under the law has been broken. Which means at the time when slavery was running rampant through this nation, and theologians of that time were preaching this message, the curse would have been made null and void because of Jesus' work at Calvary.

Let's examine another example where religion is used in the attempts to prove racial superiority. There is a group called the C.I., the Christian Identity Movement. They were formally known as the "British of Anglo-Saxon Israelism."[6] They teach that God absolutely respects persons based on their bloodline or nationality. Many of these groups are founded on anti-Semitic views claiming that white Anglo-Saxons constitute the Israel of God. They also teach that ethnic Jews are children of the devil. Like other deceived groups, theory plays a great role in their prevaricating message as they seek to use various unbiblical theories derived from scripture to support their position. They have what is called, "The Serpent Seed Theory."[7] This theory puts forth the belief that the sexual union between Adam and

Eve produced Able, the father of the Israelite or Aryan people. The people who are born into this lineage are God's children by birth; therefore there is no need for a new birth. Simply put, you come through the right seed; you need not be concerned with repentance or salvation. The theory continues with the second union between Eve and the serpent producing Cain. They believe that Cain became the father of the Jews. It was after the great flood that his descendents cohabitated with beasts, consisting of Semites, Asians and Africans, making them God's enemies.

There are a number of problems with this theory, but to hone in on the greatest dilemma with crediting this theory as fact, Dr. Alan Street says it best, "Jesus was a Jew from the tribe of Judah. Thus, according to this theory he would be the enemy of God, not the Son of God."[8]

Also, for this theory to be true, Jesus would have to contradict His own teaching in Matthew 12:25 where He discerns the thoughts of the Pharisees.[9] They heard of Jesus healing the demon possessed man who was blind and mute. And they began to speak among themselves that Jesus was driving out demons by the power of demons. And His response was, "Every kingdom divided against itself will be ruined, and every city or household divided against itself will not stand." So if you adhere to the Christian Identity Movement theory, the Jesus' statement is crazy. If indeed He was the enemy of God, then the Pharisees would have been speaking the truth. And He would have agreed with them, rather than coming against them.

I heard Dr. Tony Evans teach what is known as "The Law of First Mention." The Law of First Mention gives definition and interpretation. What this means is that if God said something in the beginning of the Bible, and He has not changed what He said at the end of the Bible, then what He said in the beginning remains. This also means we should not try to change it. That is why there are a number of things that the modern day church wants to equivocate on that we must not go with, one being the acceptance of homosexuality. The modern day church wants to accept homosexuality in response to societal pressures, but God has not changed his position on it being a sin. Let's examine these scriptures to see how this law applies to our subject and this group's theory.

> Exodus 6:7—*"And I will take you to me for a people, and I will be to you a God …"*[10]

> Deuteronomy 4:20—*"But the Lord hath taken you, and brought you forth out of the iron furnace, even out of Egypt, to be unto me a people of inheritance, as ye are this day."* [11]

> Exodus 3:7, 9, 15—*"I have surely seen the oppression of 'my' people who are in Egypt, and have heard their cry because of their taskmasters, for I know their sorrows… now, therefore, behold, the cry of the children of Israel has come to me, and I have also seen the oppression with which the Egyptians oppress them … thus you shall say to the children of Israel: 'The Lord God of your fathers, the God of Abraham, the God of Isaac, and the God of Jacob, has sent me to you. This is my name forever, and this is my memorial to all generations."*[12]

What those scriptures tell us is that the children of Israel always have been and always will be God's chosen people. When you get to the back of the Bible to the book of Revelation, you find God did not change what he said. Israel will one day awaken to the reality that Jesus is their savior according to Revelation 20-21.[13]

Now this kind of theological manipulation has also been performed on the other side of the street. There have been times when racist attitudes have come from black pastors who have also used scripture to justify their position of hatred. We saw a classic illustration of this when United States President Barack Obama's former pastor went on a racist tirade, berating white Americans, screaming from the pulpit, "God damn America!"[14]

RACISM CAN BE ROOTED IN NEGATIVE EXPERIENCES

I have a friend who admittedly struggled with any person he perceived to be Hispanic, especially Mexicans. I want to make it very clear that my friend has never been a racist, but his experience shows us how negative experiences can lead to racism if left unchecked. This aversion he had to Hispanics was born out of a negative experience from his days as a youth growing up in the Midwest. His small Midwestern town was home to a large Mexican population. As a high school student he had an altercation with a Mexican student. After that day, he grew up with an underlying fear and mistrust of Hispanic people that had an effect on him even into adulthood.

I came to know him when he hired me to be his youth pastor in what was my first position in the ministry. I remember when I was interviewing for the position he asked that I send him a picture of me and my wife. While speaking with me over the phone, he asked me if he correctly detected my wife to be of Hispanic descent. I couldn't answer directly as my wife was adopted as a baby, but nonetheless, I didn't think much of the question again until I came to know his story.

As time went on, though I knew he was not only a good man, but a godly man. His apparent struggle with people who appeared to be Hispanic became more evident with my wife in particular. It's interesting that this great man of God had no other issues with any other ethnic group. There was great diversity in his church, including many Hispanics. But due to his difficulty communicating with and relating to them, his leadership was by default mostly white or black. Over the years God delivered him from his negative view of Hispanics by placing them in direct involvement in his ministry.

Spiritual changes began to occur and a change could be seen in his treatment of my wife and Hispanic members of the church. To this day his church is a melting pot of ethnicities, cultures and skin color. His staff and board are a clear representation of the diversity of the church he leads. Back in the 1980s I was the first black staff person, yet I never noticed any difficulty with him accepting me as a minority. His singular area of racism was towards Hispanics. But by being willing to yield the root of his issue to the Lord, God not only softened his heart but gave him a genuine compassion for the Hispanic community both locally and abroad. This healing led to successful missions works in the Hispanic populated countries of Peru and Guatemala with his first trip being to Mexico. This illustration indicates that racism can be rooted in negative experiences, but that positive experiences can change the racist view.

RACISM CAN BE ROOTED IN STEREOTYPES

Stereotype is defined as "a person, group, event, or issue considered to typify or conform to an unvarying pattern or manner, lacking any individuality."[15] In the most simplistic manner it implies the idea that "once you've seen one, you've seen them all." When it comes to races of people, it implies that they're all the same, they behave the same, and they like and dislike the same things. It's the mentality that all black people or all white people look alike. It is taking all people and lumping them into one large common group, thus measuring individuals according to our stereotypical thought process.

When I was growing up, the stereotypical line of thinking from many of my white friends was that all black people like to eat collard greens and cornbread. On the contrary, I have a disdain for both. It may be because of growing up in a poor family and those were foods we ate frequently because it easily fit into the budget for a family of eight. Therefore I was overdosed on those foods. What is more amazing than the stereotype itself is the shock and offense than many of my white friends took when they learned that I didn't like such foods.

Though there is humor to that story, there is some truth as well. Every person, at some time or another, has or will judge people out of a stereotypical mindset. Where it takes a turn is when people of the same race judge one another out of the same vein that breeds racism. I must

EVERY PERSON, AT SOME TIME OR ANOTHER, HAS OR WILL JUDGE PEOPLE OUT OF A STEROTYPICAL MINDSET.

transparently acknowledge my own guilt in operating under such a mindset. In light of the Trayvon Martin shooting, I confess being a black man does not keep me from judging every young black man who comes toward me wearing a hoodie. If I am not cautious I can allow a stereotyping mindset to cause me to view every minority I see dressed a certain way as a thug. I am saddened to say that while I was grieved at the reality that yet another young black man had been gunned down with the possibility of racial motivation, a small part of me wondered if George Zimmerman was truly fearful for his life simply because of the way a young man was dressed in the dark of night.[16] It is those attitudes and stereotypes that we must allow the Holy Spirit to cleanse our hearts from. Common sense tells us that not every hood-wearing, pants-being-held-up-by-the-gluteus, shoes-untied teenager is a thug. Movies and the media have painted this stereotypical picture in such a real way that we have bought into it as the reality of all who dress this way.

I will never forget the time my wife and I entered a particular retail store. It was our day off and we were both dressed in sweatshirts, jeans and baseball caps. As we went our separate ways I noticed after about fifteen minutes everywhere I went a certain employee kept showing up in my area. I found my wife and explained to her what I was experiencing. For the next ten minutes everywhere we went, everywhere we looked, that same employee was right there. I then separated from my wife again to see what my experience would be. That employee continued to pursue me wherever I moved but my wife was no longer followed.

I went to the front of the store and asked for a manager. I explained to her what I was experiencing. She then called that employee up and confronted her with my observations, to which, in a fit of anger, she looked at me and declared, "I'm not following you!" Sadly, the manager took the employee's word. On our way out of the store another employee pulled us to the side and began to explain why. This employee, a young white man, told us we were not imagining things. He explained that the attitude of the manager is that all black men who wear caps into a store are usually up to no good. Her philosophy was that "good" black people dress up when they shop, all others are shoplifters.

So the next Sunday my wife and I went in the same store after church, dressed to the nines in my sharpest suit and most expensive tie. As we walked in, not only were we not followed, but the customer service was excellent. We also noticed that the employee who was trailing behind me a few days earlier was now trailing around another black man wearing jeans and a baseball cap. He fit the stereotype, so he was the target that day.

Another type of racism that is born out of stereotypes is what I call "Inner Circle Racism." An example of this is black on black racism where one black person judges another black person as being black on the outside but due to actions, mannerisms or vernacular they are white on the inside, making them a sellout or an Uncle Tom.[17]

This was profoundly illustrated when ESPN ran the documentary of the Michigan Wolverine's basketball team of 1992 known as the Fab Five.[18] Consisting of five freshmen, the Fab Five took the University of Michigan to two consecutive NCAA Title Games. One of the most well known and popular members of the team was Jalen Rose. His story line was great, inspirational even until he got on the subject of the 1992 Title Game against the opposing and winning team, Duke University. In the documentary Rose says:

"For me, Duke was personal. I hated Duke and I hated everything I felt Duke stood for. Schools like Duke didn't recruit players like me. I felt like they only recruited black players that were Uncle Toms."[19]

His remarks solicited a response from NBA player Grant Hill, a Duke player at that time. Sportswriter DeWayne Wickham spoke of Hill's response that Rose seemed to be saying black athletes from two parent families who went to Duke were lackeys for whites—which is what the term Uncle Tom has come to mean. Hill wrote the documentary's characterization of Duke's players was "a sad and somewhat pathetic turn of events."[20]

I remember growing up as Grant Hill grew up. I came from a stable family with both parents present. We were taught to have dignity, speak like educated people who were proud to be American and black in America equally. On many occasions my siblings and I endured being called Uncle Toms or sell outs. Both black and white friends wanted to know, "Why don't you talk blacker?" All of that ignorance is born out of a stereotypical mentality.

There is this confusion among minorities, specifically among many of my black brothers and sisters. Many endured great danger so that all black people might have the same opportunities to embrace the best education, employment and opportunities possible. Men and women, both black and white, suffered physical, mental and emotional abuse for blacks to be equal in America. Many black students were misused, abused and attacked by segregationists for daring to integrate all-white schools, even when the law supported them. History records the names of those who literally died for our right to have equal footing in America. Yet, it seems there are times when the moment a black sister or brother begins to take advantage of these opportunities they are no longer acceptable in the black community. He or she is accused of forgetting where they came from. In the eyes of blacks and whites alike, because they don't "act black," they aren't black.

This issue really hits home in the book, *He Talk Like a White Boy.* Author Joseph C. Phillips tells of a moment in his life that changed him forever.[21] It was September of 1974. He was living in Denver, Colorado, sitting in his eighth grade English class at Pace Junior High School. The class was an accelerated course taught by Mrs. Smith. He recalled class that day, in his own words, "Stands in my mind as a monument, a shrine to all that is cold and cruel in the world." He responded to the day's discussion with what he described as, "A brilliant and insightful observation on my part." After his statement a black girl raised her hand and announced to the class, "He talk like a white boy!"

In his mind he couldn't reason what this had to do with the discussion or why she had to share that opinion with the class, even if she did feel that way. Now I want you to keep in mind this is an accelerated English class. First of all, you would think that if there is such a thing as "talking like a white boy" all who are in the class would have been there because that would have been the goal, to learn to speak proper English. But what was an even greater dilemma with his account was the fact that the teacher did not correct the young lady. It would have been a prime opportunity to teach all the students in that room how easily stereotyping can become part of our attitude. Instead of seizing the opportunity to correct an erroneous line of thinking, she said, "No Laqueesha, Joseph *speaks* like a white boy. Now Laqueesha, you try." The girl went on to say, "Mrs. Smith, Joseph speaks like a white boy!" to which the teacher replied, "Very good."[22]

The stereotypical belief that to be black is to speak one way, and to be white is to speak another was cemented in the minds of those students that day. I thought, *"If as minorities we do not respect each other how can we, or should we even, expect other races to respect us?"* The tragedy is that stereotyping is what defines "blackness" to many white people as well as black people. Phillips makes this powerful statement that I relate to with such a connection that I feel as though it is my own:

> "The man I am today has its genesis in that moment. In that instant I became acutely aware that I was different. Until that moment, I never realized there was something wrong with the way I spoke, that answering a question in class was acting 'white.' I never knew how ugly or hurtful the words 'Uncle Tom' were. In that moment of tyranny of opinion—the notion that there are some people empowered to stand at the doors of culture and determine who and who is not welcome—was made painfully clear to me. My definition of blackness—more accurately, my black self—was unimportant. That decision was left to the anointed, and no matter how idiotic, arcane, or nihilistic their definition, any deviation would be dealt with swiftly and decisively."[23]

Think with me for a moment. The evil of racism is so strong that even those who want out from under the label and inequities racism has placed on them will hold on to a measure of that which identifies them with that from which they have fought to be delivered from. While racism can be rooted in stereotypes, all races must understand that we must respect ourselves before we can expect others to respect us, and we must respect each other before we can demand others to respect us. This is true for all mankind from all walks of life, both male and female. But I contend that for blacks in America it is more so.

What I share next will probably upset some of my sisters and brothers, as it did when Bill Cosby made these statements. I confess, some of his words made me cringe as well, but are nonetheless true. My prayer is that his words encourage a greater level of self respect and dignity in all minorities. It is called "We Cannot Blame the White People Any Longer." Here are some excerpts of his remarks:

> "People marched and were hit in the face with rocks to get an education, now we've got these knuckleheads walking around talking like they've never been in a classroom in their lives …We have to start holding each other to a higher standard. We can't blame the white people any longer … It is time for us ladies and gentlemen, to look at the numbers. Fifty percent of our children are dropping out of high school. Sixty percent of the incarcerated males happen to be illiterate. There's a correlation. Tell the media to stop asking me what I think about people who don't believe what I'm saying or feel that I'm too harsh or feel that I'm just running my mouth because I'm old. Think about this for a minute: seventy percent of the pregnant teenagers happen to be African American girls. They didn't impregnate themselves."[24]

What Bill Cosby is saying in my mind's eye is that as minorities we must first respect one another before we demand respect from others.

My experience as a black man has been that all black people want to get ahead, but like any other people, not all black people are willing to pay the price. And if you are, you must be prepared to be stereotyped by some who see your advancements as you being a sellout. We must learn to build one another up and not tear down. For, we cannot strengthen the weak while seeking to weaken the strong. I believe that Spike Lee said it well:

> "We have to work harder so these young minds understand that they cannot equate acting intelligent with acting white ... there is nothing cute about being ignorant."

RACISM CAN BE ROOTED IN MYTHS

One definition of a myth is "fiction or half-truth, especially one that forms part of the ideology of a society." Another definition is "somebody or something whose existence is widely believed in, but who is fictitious." [25]

Out of this is many times born "mythical" thinking. Meaning something is not true or real, but only existing in somebody's imagination. Another way of looking at this is a story that has not one ounce of truth to it, but when it is told often enough people begin to accept it as factual.

Every ethnic group has certain things that are indicative to them. The fact of the matter is this: I am a minority, and many of my minority friends of various ethnicities agree that our experience has been that there is a tendency in a great number of minority groups to be "late" for appointments. I have many friends and church members who are considered to be minorities in this country, and the one commonality I find in each group is that they are notoriously late for appointments. My assistant pastor is Puerto Rican and many of my church leaders are Haitian or African and we often joke about operating on CP time, or "colored people time." Now is that true of all minorities? Of course not. But it does not deny the reality that this is a common quality in members of many minority groups. This commonality justifies the belief of many that this is true of all minorities. But I stand myself as an exception to the presumed rule because I am a minority yet I hold the position, "If you are early you are on time, if you are on time you are late, and if you are late, don't bother coming." I am consistently pestering my family not to make us late; for my belief is when a person is consistently late it is a lack of respect for other people's time.

Let me illustrate the danger of myths in a more drastic way. On January 16, 1988 *Sports Illustrated* ran an article concerning one of my favorite football analysts Jimmy Snyder. The headline for the story read, "Jimmy 'The Greek' Snyder Canned for 'Racist' Remarks." He was fired after twelve years as a CBS analyst for remarks he made to a Washington, D.C. television reporter concerning the physical abilities of black and white athletes. It is reported that Snyder said:

> "The black is a better athlete to begin with because he's been bred to be that way, because of his high thighs and big thighs that goes up his back and they jump higher and run faster because of their bigger thighs and he's bred to be the better athlete because this goes all the way back to the civil war when during the slave trade'n the big ... the owner ... the slave owner would, would, would, would breed his big black to his big black woman so that he could have ah, ah big, ah big, ah big black kid see ..."[26]

According to the New York Times obituary, Snyder expressed regret for his comments, remarking, "What a foolish thing to say."[27]

Now, here's the part that is most troubling. It is reported that while his CBS workers purportedly supported the theory privately, they couldn't admit it publicly and decided it was best for CBS to fire him. There are those who testified that they knew Snyder for a long time and they never heard any racist comments nor detected any racist attitudes from him. Please don't miss the sadness of this story. I repeat, it is alleged that behind the scenes, those who fired him also believed the myth. I do not believe Jimmy believing such a myth made him a racist, but I do believe there are many out there with racist attitudes because of belief in such myths.

As I mentioned earlier, my wife was adopted. The family she was adopted into was a white family of Dutch descent. My wife on the contrary was a dark skinned, beautiful little girl with exotic features and stunning green eyes. Being adopted by a white family was not a problem, as I believe people should adopt whomever they desire. However, problems did arise out of the obvious differences as she grew up in a mostly white town in a very "white" family.

One of her Christian school teachers told her that adoption was unbiblical and that her parents were wrong for adopting her. She would come home from school crying, telling her mother the horrible names the kids would call her. The only response she received from her parents was that they were Dutch and because they adopted her she was Dutch. They also told her that she could not possibly be black because black people did not have green eyes. Needless to say their response did nothing to solve the problem or lesson the pain. But God has such a great sense of humor. One day an insurance salesman showed up at her parent's doorstep. When her mother opened the door she got the shock of her life. Standing in front of her was a very dark skinned black man with curly hair and blue eyes.

What we have to understand is that myths are many times born out of lies and misleading information. One of the myths that was used to substantiate racism was that black people and other minorities were inferior and incapable of learning at the level of the white race among others. Here are a few myths shattering statistics about minorities:

- **Myth**: Black women are more suited to help than educated.

- **Truth**: There are a greater percentage of black women enrolled in college than other races.[28]

  - Black Women: 9.4%
  - Asian Women: 9.2%
  - White Women: 7.1%
  - Hispanic Women: 6.2%

- **Myth**: Young black men are more engaged in crime than education.

- **Truth**: There are more black men in college than in prison.[29]

  - Black Men in Prison (18-24): 164,000
  - Black Men in College (18-24): 674,000
  - Total Black Men in Prison: 824,340
  - Total Black Men in College: 1,444,979

Why is this information important? Even the media paints and perpetuates myths for us through false information. And when we hear the myths long enough we begin to not only believe them, we fight to hold on to them. Even as a black man, I myself believed for years there were more young black men in prison than in college. It took some time for me to break through that mythological thought pattern. Franz Fannon makes this observation:

> "Sometimes people hold a core belief that is very strong. When they are presented with evidence that works against that belief, the new evidence cannot be accepted. It would create a feeling that is extremely uncomfortable, called cognitive dissonance. And because it is so important to protect the core belief, they will rationalize, ignore and even deny anything that doesn't fit in with their core belief."[30]

I had friends who tried to discourage me from going out for cross country in high school. My white and black friends both told me there was not only no way I would make the team, but I would certainly never reach my goal of being the number one runner on the team. Their belief was rooted in the myth we had been taught for years that black people were not built to run long distances. We were told black people have short muscles that make us more suitable to sports like basketball, football and sprinting events in track. White people on the contrary were more suited for long distances because of their long lean muscles. It was interesting to me that even after I won the number one runner trophy and made honorable mention all-conference, many of my friends said it was a fluke. They said what I had accomplished was not normal and would probably never happen again.

A couple of years later, not only did one of my younger brothers successfully break my records, but he went on to receive a partial scholarship for cross country and track. In addition, there is no denying the greatest distance runners in the world, including the marathon, are mostly African. The Boston Marathon supports this fact in that in the last twenty-five years twenty-three out of twenty-five winners in the men's division have been of African descent and likewise, fourteen of the last sixteen in the women's division have been of African descent.[31]

Let me cite two more examples, less we think that myths only come from what white people believe about black people. In the 1992 movie *White Men Can't Jump,* the obvious element was to disprove that myth which was birthed out of a belief many people adhered to. Many years prior to that movie coming out I was in junior college and there was a farm boy on my basketball team who disproved that myth one day in practice. Dave, who was just over six feet tall, took two basketballs, put one in each hand, stood under the basket, jumped straight up and dunked both balls at the same time, thus disproving the myth that white men can't jump. This was an amazing feat because neither I nor my black friends had ever met a white guy who could dunk one basketball, forget about two!

One more myth from the opposite side of the race issue thrives to this day, though it has been disproven. The story has circulated for years and can be found in references such as *The International Library of Afro-American Life and History* (1978), and the 1981 *Encyclopedia of Black Americans*.[32] The myth is that the creator of the blood bank, a black man, died after an automobile accident when he was refused lifesaving treatment at a southern hospital simply because he was black. The myth gained steam when

William Loren Katz wrote this in his 1967 book, *Eye Witness: The Negro in American History:*

> "On April 1, 1950, Dr. Drew was injured in an auto accident near Burlington, North Carolina. Although he was bleeding profusely, he was turned from the nearest white hospital. By the time he was taken to another hospital the scientist had bled to death."[33]

Some of the other avenues through which this myth has spread include Dick Gregory who told it in his monologues and Isaac Asimov, who included this information in his first edition of his *Book of Facts*.[34] This myth has such strength of popularity that it even made its way into an episode of the television series *M*A*S*H*. It is told by the character Hawkeye Pierce played by Alan Alda.[35] But it didn't stop there. Musician Wynton Marsalis also repeated the story in a 1987 segment of the television series *57th Street*.[36]

When Dr. John R. Ford, a passenger in the car, was interviewed by Scot Morris of *Omni Magazine*, what he describes disputes the myth:

> "He had a superior vena cava syndrome—blood was blocked getting back to his heart from his brain and upper extremities. To give him a transfusion would have killed him sooner."

The 1989 edition of *The Negro Almanac*, as with most current reference works, not only shoots a hole in the myth but also puts the truth at the forefront when it states, "Dr. Drew was killed in an automobile crash."[37]

Though many times these myths can be funny, I have found that even in church circles we believe some of the mythical nonsense we have heard down through the years. I grew up in a church environment where a white pastor would never be allowed to preach because it was believed they didn't have enough "soul" to keep the attention of the black audience. I grew up believing that you didn't even have to look at the man, all you had to do was hear the voice and you would be able to discern whether the preacher was black or white. I believed that myth until the day I heard the late R.W. Shambach and Pastor Rod Parsley break the Bread of Life.

One Sunday I sat on the kitchen barstool studying as my wife cooked dinner. She had the television turned on to a man preaching under a heavy anointing. At that time I had lost interest in most television preachers for my own personal reasons. Suddenly she realized what she was listening to in my presence and quickly switched the channel. I asked her what she was doing and to please turn back to the man who was preaching. I hadn't heard preaching like that in such a long time as he was unusually anointed. I must confess I was momentarily stunned when I realized the man was Rod Parsley of World Harvest Church in Columbus, Ohio. That was my first, and thank God, not my last encounter with his ministry. It was also my first experience hearing a white man preach with a style, if you will, that I had been taught could only be found in black preachers.

RACISM CAN BE ROOTED IN IGNORANCE

Ignorance means 1) without education or knowledge; 2) exhibiting lack of education or knowledge; 3) unaware or misinformed.

Sometimes people are behaving in a racist manner without even realizing they are doing so. Now myths can breed ignorance and vice versa, but ignorance can also happen because of a lack of understanding. I was sitting in the Dallas/Fort Worth Airport with my family awaiting a return flight home to Boston. My oldest daughter was sitting in a section next to a couple who were waiting to board the same flight. In the meantime the wife made a phone call where the other person apparently asked her if she got any sun. She responded, "I've had so much sun I look like I'm part Negro," with added laughter. Her husband looked uncomfortable as the woman glanced in my daughter's direction with a smile on her face because she was obviously unable to comprehend for one moment that her statement could have been offensive. The impression I got as I walked over to the area and sat for a few moments was this woman had no intention of trying to be offensive and would likely be offended if someone insinuated she was a racist.

It was clear the husband was highly embarrassed as he tried unsuccessfully to get her to hang up the phone. The poor man was turning red as an apple, but it did not prevent her from continuing to make racially insensitive remarks. I do not doubt that she regularly talks that way. But what she doesn't understand is her remarks were made out of ignorance in that she was making those remarks in the presence of someone black. Apparently she did not understand that black people do not go by "Negro" any more. Neither did she understand that we do not find it complimentary when someone equates enjoying the sun and getting a tan to being "part Negro."

... HER REMARKS WERE MADE OUT OF IGNORANCE ...

Then there was the occasion in high school when one of my white friends and I were having a conversation about hair. It stunned me when he piped up and said, "Well, you don't have much trouble in the morning with your hair. All you have to do is get up and pat it a little bit and it falls into place." Now this was in the days of the afro hairdo. Having straight hair, he never had to care for one of those big fellas. If he had, he would know that it takes a whole lot more effort than a pat on the head to shape it just right. But the clincher came when he stated it has to be much easier because black people only wash their hair once a week anyway. He was the same friend who informed me that black people should only date black people and white people should only date white people because the Bible speaks out against the "mixin' of the races." That is racism born out of ignorance.

Once again I will state that racism is not one sided. I will never forget the day I took the beautiful woman, now my wife, home from college one weekend to meet my parents. My father's sisters had learned prior to our visit from my parents that my wife was a very bright skinned woman. When they found out we had arrived, it didn't take them but two minutes to make the drive to my parent's home. We were sitting at the dining room table and upon their arrival they proceeded to walk past me without even speaking. Circling my wife like buzzards, they walked around her several times, examining, looking her up and down. Finally one of my aunts touched her hair and stated, "Oh yeah! She's got some of us in her. She's one of us." In other words, she passed the test to date me because she at least had *some* black in her which was proved by the texture of her hair. The problem is that they did not realize that they were being racist out of ignorance. I relate again to my wife being adopted. She has no idea who her biological parents are.

The records are sealed by law in the state of Washington where she was adopted. Unless the birth mother makes the first step to open communication, she has no access to her records. Imagine the pain someone like my wife has had to endure because of people who operate in a racist mentality rooted in ignorance.

Countless times she has had to field the questions, "What are you? Are you a mix of this or that?" When she responds that she doesn't know, many do not accept that as an acceptable answer. They respond with the challenging question of "How can you not know?" She now gives an answer that I think is a wonderful rebuttal. She simply says, "I am whatever you want me to be. I am racially ambiguous!" I think how sad it is that any person should have to defend their ethnicity to those who call Jesus Savior and Lord. The Body of Christ must lead the way and begin to look at people through spirit eyes and not natural, fleshy eyes. And greater yet, we must seek to avoid operating in ignorance.

RACISM CAN BE ROOTED IN OUTSIDE INFLUENCE

Racially based hatred is a learned response. No one is born into this world with the desire to hate another simply because there is a difference in the color of their skin. In my pastorate of a multi-ethnic church I am allowed the wonderful experience and privilege of dedicating children of so many different ethnic backgrounds. Because of this diversity I have dedicated babies of African, Haitian, Caribbean, and Hispanic descent. I have also dedicated many white babies as many of our congregants are of Irish or Italian descent. I have never had one child look at me with fear in their eyes or hatred because their pastor is a black man. Those very children will one day grow up, and the day will come that racism will have no place in their hearts *if* their parents teach them by example to judge people by their character rather than by the color of their skin. Children become what they are taught. I grew up with an inclination to love everybody because my parents never taught me that I was different than my white friends living next door or across the street from me, nor were they different from me. Matter of fact, I wasn't even aware growing up in the 1960s of the struggles for equality that were raging in this nation. I didn't know there were places in the south where blacks and whites had separate drinking fountains, and if you were black you could not stay in certain hotels. I was naïve to the fact that even in my little northern town just west of Chicago, there were white people who didn't want black people living in their neighborhoods. I didn't know that when my best friend who was white would get mad at me and call me "nicko" he was really calling me a nigger. In my child innocence I thought he was just calling me something he called his brothers or sisters when he got mad. My parents never taught me to hate people because of their skin color, so I didn't understand why some of my black friends hated my white friends and vice versa. I had never seen my white friends do anything to harm them nor my black friends towards my white friends. But as I grew older I began to understand that my friend calling me "nicko" and the animosity that existed between my black and white friends shared one common value. They had been taught racist attitudes by their racist parents.

I am not alone when it comes to what I would call the bliss of ignorance. Even those who grew up in families who were fighting for freedom shared a measure of shelter from the storms of racism.

Dexter Scott King, son of the great late Dr. Martin Luther King, Jr., shares a similar experience growing up.[38] He tells of a childhood in which, though he knew his father was involved in something great, his siblings early on were not aware of how some hated them simply because of the darkness of their skin. He describes this point in his life in his own words:

> "As children, we didn't know we were 'Negroes,' or if we did, we didn't exactly know what that meant. We didn't realize we lived in 'segregation,' didn't know there were better pools than the one we crowded into at the Y, or that we and our friends would be considered 'have-nots' if our father wasn't the co-pastor of Ebenezer Baptist Church. We weren't aware that we could and would be turned away from public accommodations, educational institutions, or turned away from desirable living spaces by the real estate restrictive covenants. We weren't aware that we were shunned by society, murdered over mere glances, made to feel less than human. We were children, and children are more than human; we were blessed, but sooner or later we'd grow up and have to face this prison of segregation, unless daddy won his struggle."[39]

Dr. King didn't just preach non-violent resistance. He raised his children in an environment that fostered love even for those whom they would someday come to learn hated them. While we all have the potential to hate because of the sinful nature, no one is born with a hate-filled heart. We must be taught to hate. Though many people have the ability to put on a loving act in public, the truth is, the hate that exists behind closed doors is many times revealed through their children.

I will never forget a single mother who served as a youth worker with my wife and me when I was a youth pastor at First Assembly of God in Worcester, MA. This church and youth group were predominately white as were most of my youth workers, including this single mother. She had a young daughter, around four years of age. Her daughter would fight going to the children's class until her mother allowed her to "go see God!" Her mother told her God is everywhere and you can't see Him with the natural eye. However that was not enough to satisfy this young girl's curiosities. She struggled each week to get her into that class until one week she brought her into youth group. The little girl ran up to me and said, "Hi God!" That little girl didn't care about the color of my skin. All she recognized was that I had something to do with God and in her little understanding I must "be" God.

There are two things I learned from that experience. The first is her mother was apparently teaching her something right because that small child would run and jump in my arms as though I were a father to her. The second lesson I learned was that when we behave as the church should behave when it comes to all relationships our children will not only do as we do but as we say.

Proverbs 22:6 says, "Train up a child in the way he should go: and when he is old, he will not depart from it."[40] The phrase "train up" means to initiate and to inaugurate.[41] It means to direct and influence the direction a child should go in. And even in his old age he will still follow the direction he was taught as a child. Another translation reads this way: "Point your kids in the right direction—when they're old they won't be lost."[42] While the secular world may believe in the influence of many outside forces, God's Word declares that the greatest influence in children's lives are parents. The words "train up" infer influence, both by what we say and what we do.

RACISM CAN BE ROOTED IN THE FALSE BELIEFS

There is a false teaching that indicates more than one human race actually exists. This is an area that is a delicate line upon which to walk, but it is necessary to do so in order to approach racism with a proper perspective. When people use the word "race" they are speaking to a man's thoughts when it comes to the color of people's skin and other physical external features. While there is no disputing that there are various differences in outward appearances among human beings, it is my contention that the word "race" is a man created label that is used to create a human explanation and justification for one group seeking domination and superiority over another.

It is more about the social than the biological. I agree with Paul R. Spickard when he says, "It is my contention ... however, that race while it has relationship to biology, is not mainly a biological matter. Race is primarily a sociopolitical construct. The sorting of people into this race or that in the modern day era has generally been done by powerful groups for the purpose of maintaining and extending their own power."[43] In essence, there is ultimately no biological basis for the use of the word "race" when speaking of human beings.

The word race actually means, "of a common stock, to be born of the same class,"[44] and "a group of persons who come from the same ancestor."[45] If you truly define creation biblically, there is really no such thing as races of people. Science supports this reality. Biologically there are different ethnicities, nationalities, cultures, but only one race, the human race. [46] There is nonsense out there stating there are different races that has been touted as truth.

It has been said there is black blood, white blood, Indian blood, Hispanic blood, Asian blood or you name it blood. The most ridiculous falsehood stemming from this theory, in my estimation, is the belief that if you have one drop of "black blood" in you you are black. If the father is black, then you are "officially" black. This causes confusion in situations when the father is white but the mother is black as when female slaves were raped by white men and produced a child that was then considered black as well. It is important that we understand that while there are different blood types in terms of the presence of antibodies and antigens it is still human blood running through every person's veins. But blood type has nothing to do with race, nationality or ethnicity. If that were the case then all white people, all blacks, all Hispanics, all Asians would possess the same blood type as pertains to their racial grouping. This would also mean it would not be possible for persons mixed with two or more ethnic backgrounds to exist. But this is how racism can blind people to the degree that some would rather lose their life than accept blood from someone of a "different race."

In the April 23, 2013 *Paul's Justice Page*, the story is told of Hans Serelman who was a doctor in Germany in 1935. One of his patients was in need of a blood transfusion. Blood transfusions at that time were done by finding a live donor rather than stored blood. When a suitable donor was not able to be found quickly enough, Dr. Serelman opened his own artery and donated his blood. Sadly, the doctor was not thanked but was instead sent to a concentration camp for defiling the blood of the German race by using his "Jewish" blood to save a life.[47]

Even more tragic was that from the one act of compassion, Germany began to eliminate the "Jewish Influence" from medicine by limiting Jews' access to patients and medical school. What was driving this movement? It was the idea that Aryan supremacy needed to be understood clearly, and the tool by which to do so was a study of blood that would distinguish Aryans from Jews. Hatred, and particularly racial hatred, will drive people to seek to prove their position of perceived superiority, even at their own expense. The Germans barred more than 8,000 Jewish doctors from practice and replaced them with hastily trained and inexperienced paramedics. With this, "the infusion of mythology and misapplied anthropology set back serious scientific research on blood." The Nuremberg Blood Protection Laws severely limited the availability of blood transfusions because of the possibility of being charged with an "attack on German blood" if the donor could not prove it was pure Aryan blood.[48]

At the same time, this war was also an issue in the United States. We have heard in this country the usage of the terms "colored" versus "white" blood. *Paul's Justice Page* states, "The Red Cross knew that 'blood was blood' and did not differ by race, but followed the wishes of the military and refused to collect blood from African Americans."[49] After the attack on Pearl Harbor there was a large demand for blood to treat the many wounded soldiers. But what is so sad is that while blood was collected from blacks, their blood was labeled and processed separately. A *New York Times* editorial made this observation:

"The prejudice against Negro blood for transfusions is all the more difficult to understand because many a southerner was nursed at the breast of a Negro nanny ... sometimes we wonder whether this is really an age of science."

Racism is so deceiving that in the late 1950s Arkansas passed a law requiring the segregation of blood. This segregation only came to an end during the 1960s, more due to force because of the civil rights movement than the continued advances in science.

In another account, AARP, Real Possibilities, Blair S. Walker reported "Patient Refuses Caregiver's Help Because of Race." In the Plainfield Healthcare Center nursing home in Indianapolis, Indiana, resident Marjorie Latshow had fallen. Employee Brenda Chaney's immediate impulse was to help the woman up. Instead the elderly woman refused her help because she was black. Thus, Brenda, a certified nursing assistant had to hastily locate a white worker, because this fallen and helpless patient had stated in writing that she wanted nothing to do with black nursing assistants. It is also alleged that Brenda Chaney was demeaned by her supervisors at the suburban Indianapolis nursing home with written reminders not to enter the room of Marjorie Latshow and provide her with care. Needless to say, Brenda filed a lawsuit, but the importance of this story is how racism has the power to so blind people that they would even endanger their very lives to defend it.[50]

Let's use one of God's lower creations to teach a little lesson. Let me go back to one of the definitions of race: "of a common stock." Cows would be from a common stock. You see a cow is a cow is a cow is a cow. All that a cow will ever be is a cow. As a child my wife grew up on a dairy farm and what I have come to learn from her is that there are different breeds of cattle. There are Brahman,

Hereford, Texas Longhorn, Holsteins, Angus, Black, Red and Tan Angus and dozens more. There is a way to identify different breeds of cows, yet they are all cows. If I may put it into context, there are different "ethnicities" of cows yet the cows all belong to one "race." Within each breed or "ethnicity" there are various common characteristics. Dairy cattle are generally angular and wedged in shape with large noticeable udders. Beef cows on the other hand are rectangular, stocky and muscular. When you look at the various cows you should take notice of the color and markings of the cattle. Colors include black, white, red, brown, dun and various combinations. Markings can occur as belts, spots, or shadings. There can be differences in nose color and facial markings. The texture of the coat or hair can vary including curly, shaggy, smooth, sleek, long or short. These diverse qualities serve distinct purposes. Long, shaggy hair common in the northern breeds protects the cattle from cold damp weather. A short sleek coat allows rapid cooling for those in warm climates. There are also differences in the length of the horns. Pottle cattle are hornless. Depending on the breed, pottle are natural or mechanical. Crossbreeds have several different types of cattle in their ancestry.[51] After looking at more than one breed and identifying the differences among each one, the conclusion is clear—they are all cows. It doesn't matter what the cow looks like, the breed or "ethnicity" of the cow, the cow is a cow is a cow ... and all a cow ever will be is a cow.

The fact that a cow is crossbred does not change the fact that it is a cow. It has different features but it is still from a common stock, from one family. How much more then when two people of different ethnicities procreate and have children that the same holds true? For years, and even today, there are those who refer to a child born to a Native American and a white person as a "half-breed!" The features of the children show a combination of both parents, yet they are still of a common stock. If race indeed means "common stock" then there cannot be races within races.

IF RACE INDEED MEANS "COMMON STOCK" THEN THERE CANNOT BE RACES WITHIN RACES.

A similar comparison can be made with cars. One vehicle may be a Chevrolet and another Mercedes Benz. But they are still both cars. They are different models in terms of appearance and performance ability but it is still a car. You wouldn't call it anything else. This theory of separate races is interesting because there are not many people left on this people planet who do not have some "racial mix" in them. As Paul R. Spickard states, "What is a person of mixed race? Biologically speaking, we are all mixed. That is, we all have genetic material from a variety of populations, and we all exhibit physical characteristics that testify to mixed ancestry. Biologically speaking, there never have been any pure races—all populations are mixed."[52] Dexter King's paternal grandfather, Mike King, born in 1899 was born to Delia Lindsey and James Albert King whose father was a white Irishman.[53] Even in my own family we have pictures of great aunts and uncles who could pass as white today.

Races of people is a label that man came up with in order to support their evil desire to exalt one group of people over another. The Bible does not distinguish between races in terms of people. Revelation 14 speaks of the scene that is looking to the end of the great tribulation. Verse 6 reads:

> "And I saw another angel fly in the midst of heaven, having the everlasting gospel to preach unto them that dwell on earth, and to every nation, and kindred, tongue, and people."[54]

The words "nation," "tongue," and "people are key in that they all point to one thing. The realization that there will be people gathered on that day from many nations, speaking many different languages, but that is their only distinction. The word "people" in this context is the Greek word *"Laos"* referring to the common people.[55] The word "nation" is the Greek word *"ethno"* meaning the whole race of mankind.[56] The apostle Paul often used that same word to make only one distinction in mankind. Paul's use of the word "nation" or "ethnos" was also used when distinguishing gentiles from heathens, or believers from unbelievers. The point that must be driven home is that God's only focus is to distinguish mankind in the area of believer and unbeliever. Some believe the angel spoken of in this passage will be the Gospel message preached over the airwaves that all will be able to hear simultaneously. I believe it will be the voice of one of God's angels. On that day in Revelation everyone will have not only the same need for the Gospel in common, and though representing many ethnic groups, they will be of the same race, the human race. What a fearful day that will be for those who refuse to repent and receive God's amazing grace.

The deepest of the roots of racism is a problem called "foolish pride." Every person needs to have pride. The problem is when that pride turns foolish we become blind to reality. Foolish pride has gotten many people physically killed, but it also kills spiritually. Foolish pride is the spirit that causes one group of people to seek to exalt themselves over another group. I heard Dr. John Maxwell share the following quote from John Seldon who said it best:

> "Pride may be allowed to this or that degree; otherwise a man cannot keep his dignity. In gluttony there must be eating. In

drunkenness there must be drinking. It's not the eating, nor the drinking that is to be blamed, but the excess. So it is with pride."[57]

Foolish pride infects all of us in some way, at some time. The problem with the Body of Christ is not that we should avoid pride. The problem is when foolish pride is allowed to rear its ugly head. And that makes us dangerous. And where does foolish pride come from in the life of a Christian? It is when our heads are filled with knowledge of who Christ is and His word but our hearts are not mutually filled with the knowledge of who Christ is and His word.

ENDNOTES

1. *The Maxwell Leadership Bible* (New King James Version). Nashville, Tennessee: Thomas Nelson Bibles, 2002.
2. *The Hebrew-Greek Key Study Bible* (King James Version). Edited By Spiros Zodhiates, Th.D. Chattanooga, Tennessee: AMG Publishers, 1984, 1991. Print.
3. *The Maxwell Leadership Bible* (New King James Version). Nashville, Tennessee: Thomas Nelson Bibles, 2002.
4. Dodds, Elreta. *The Trouble with Farrakhan and the Nation of Islam*. Detroit, Michigan: Press Toward the Mark Publications, 1997, 2000.
5. Edited by Rex Humbard Ministries. *Prophecy Bible Edition (The New King James Version)*. Akron, Ohio: Thomas Nelson, Inc., 1985.
6. *The Apologetics Study Bible*. Edited by Ted Cabal. Nashville, Tennessee: Holman Bible Publishers, 2007. Print.
7. Ibid.
8. Ibid.
9. The Hebrew-Greek Key Study Bible (King James Version). Edited By Spiros Zodhiates, Th.D. Chattanooga, Tennessee: AMG Publishers, 1984, 1991. Print.
10. Ibid.
11. Ibid.
12. *The Maxwell Leadership Bible* (New King James Version). Nashville, Tennessee: Thomas Nelson Bibles, 2002.
13. Ibid.
14. Ebony Editors. "Scandalous." Ebony. March 2013: 119-129. Print.

15. *The American Heritage Dictionary.* Second Edition. Boston, Massachusetts: Houghton Mifflin Company, 1982, 1985. Print.

16. Alvarez, Lizette. "Justice Department Investigation is Sought in Florida Teenager's Shooting Death." *New York Times* (Reprints). 16 March 2012. Web. 17 April 2013.

17. *The American Heritage Dictionary.* Second Edition. Boston, Massachusetts: Houghton Mifflin Company, 1982, 1985. Print.

18. Wickman, DeWayne. "Jalen Rose Needs to Take Back 'Uncle Tom' Jab." USA Today 22 March 2011: 7A. Print.

19. Ibid.

20. Ibid.

21. Phillips, Joseph C. *He Talk Like a White Boy.* Philadelphia, Pennsylvania: Running Press, 2006.

22. Ibid.

23. Ibid.

24. Cosby, Dr. William Henry "Bill", Jr. *We Cannot Blame the White People Any Longer.* California Indian Education. Web. 14 June 2013.

25. *The American Heritage Dictionary.* Second Edition. Boston, Massachusetts: Houghton Mifflin Company, 1982, 1985. Print.

26. Cosmell, Howard. "10 Ridiculously Racist Remarks from Sports Personalities." *Total Pro Sports.* 7 October 2010. Web. 3 May 2013.

27. Pace, Eric. "Jimmy (The Greek) Snyder, 76, Is Dead." *The New York Times*: Obituaries. 22 April 1996. Web. 3 May 2013.

28. "Dispelling the Myth." *What Black Men Think: Ten Days of Black Truths.* Web. 26 June 2013.

29. Ibid.

30. Fanon, Frantz. *Black Skin, White Masks.* Translated by Richard Philcox. New York, New York: Grove Press, 1967, 2008.

31. Luciano, Michael. Boston Marathon Winners: Full List. Policy Mic: Culture, Sports. 2012. Web. 22 April 2013.

32. Brunvand, Jan Harold. "Black Creator of Blood Bank Wasn't Denied Treatment." *Deseret News.* 24 May 1991. Web. 23 April 2013.

33. Ibid.

34. Ibid.

35. Ibid.

36. Ibid.

37. Ibid.

38. King, Dexter Scott; Wiley, W. Ralph. *Growing Up King.* New York, New York: Warner Books, 2003.

39. Ibid.

40. *The Hebrew-Greek Key Study Bible* (King James Version). Edited By Spiros Zodhiates, Th.D. Chattanooga, Tennessee: AMG Publishers, 1984, 1991. Print.

41. Ibid.

42. *The Message* (Numbered Edition). Ed. Eugene H. Peterson. Colorado Springs, Colorado: Navpress, 2005. Print.

43. Spickard, Paul R. "Mixed Race America—The Illogic of America Racial Categories." PBS. Web. 23 April 2013.

44. *Webster's Dictionary.* 2003 Edition. Print.

45. *Webster's New Explorer Thesaurus.* New Edition. 2005. Print.

46. Schaefer, Richard T. *Racial & Ethnic Groups.* Upper Saddle River, New Jersey: Pearson Prentice Hall, 2004.

47. Leighton, Paul. *Class, Race, Gender and Crime: Social Realities of Justice in America – Box 3.1 Race & Blood.* 2000. Paul's Justice Page. 23 April 2013.

48. Ibid.

49. Ibid.

50. Walker, Blair S. "Patient Refuses Caregivers Help Because of Race." *AARP Real Possibilities.* 22 September 2010. Web. 23 April 2013.

51. North American Dairy Breeds—Breeds of Livestock. Oklahoma State University Board of Regents. 1997. Web. 23 April 2013.

52. Spickard, Paul R. "Mixed Race America—The Illogic of America Racial Categories."PBS. Web. 23 April 2013.

53. King, Dexter Scott; Wiley, W. Ralph. *Growing Up King.* New York, New York: Warner Books, 2003

54. *The Hebrew-Greek Key Study Bible* (King James Version). Edited By Spiros Zodhiates, Th.D. Chattanooga, Tennessee: AMG Publishers, 1984, 1991. Print.

55. Ibid.

56. Ibid.

57. *The Maxwell Leadership Bible* (New King James Version). Nashville, Tennessee: Thomas Nelson Bibles, 2002.

RACES OF PEOPLE IS A LABEL THAT
MAN CAME UP WITH IN ORDER TO
SUPPORT THEIR EVIL DESIRE TO EXALT
ONE GROUP OF PEOPLE OVER ANOTHER.
THE BIBLE DOES NOT DISTINGUISH
BETWEEN RACES IN TERMS OF PEOPLE.

CHAPTER THREE

RACISM IS A SPIRITUAL PROBLEM

RACISM IS ROOTED IN SATAN'S DESIRE

It must be understood: racism is ultimately a spiritual problem rooted in Satan's desire to keep the church of Jesus Christ divided, dysfunctional and delayed from her destiny. The church must recognize that at the very core, racism is driven by demonic forces. Its power can only be broken by spiritual force working through men.

Matthew 16:13-19 records, "When Jesus came to the region of Caesarea Philippi, He asked His disciples, 'Who do men say that I, the Son of Man, am?' So they said, 'Some say John the Baptist, some Elijah, and others Jeremiah or one of the prophets.'"[1] Jesus told His disciples that He heard His name was being talked about around town. He inquired what was being said about Him asking, "Tell me, what is my reputation around town?" Notice Jesus did not say, "Come on boys, why didn't you stop them and tell them who I really am?" The next thing He asks is, "But what about you? Who do you say that I am?" You see, Jesus really didn't care about what the people out there thought about Him. What He wanted to know was what His disciples thought about Him. What did those who were closest to Him and knew Him the best think about Him?

The question remains the same for the church today. He wants to know what we think about who He is. Who do we really believe the Son of God is? Sometimes the church is too busy lambasting the world, talking poorly about government officials, criticizing the president and the White House for the condition of the nation and the world. Every four years we are in an uproar about who's going to be in the White House. While we should care, we should not be fearful no matter who sits in the Oval Office, for we are connected to the One who promised He would never leave us or forsake us. Jesus' question to the disciples on that day translates into our present time because He is not concerned about what those in the White House think about Him. His greatest concern is what do those of us who attend the church house think of Him.

In response to that question, Peter answered in verse 16, "You are the Christ, the Son of the Living God."[2] When Peter made this declaration, Jesus spoke words that opened the door of the first revelation of how God would use the church in His redemption plan for man. Jesus response to Peter was, "Blessed are you, Simon Bar-Jonah, for flesh and blood has not revealed this to you, but my father who is in heaven." Jesus spoke this to Peter, but His response was directed to all the disciples.

If you follow the Gospels it is evident that Peter was the spokesman, the leader, "the rock" as Jesus referred to him. When Jesus responded to Peter's answer He was not only speaking to

Peter, He was speaking to the rest of the disciples and to the church of Jesus Christ—every subsequent disciple who would come after those original disciples.

Here is where we find the first reference to the church. Jesus' words that day were spoken in revelation toward all future disciples, meaning all who are saved by faith. He declared it is through that revelation given to Peter by the Holy Spirit on that day. It is through the revelation of who He is that He will build His church and He promises that the gates of Hades will not prevail against it. In Matthew 16:19 Jesus speaks these powerful words "And I will give you the keys to the kingdom of heaven, and whatever you bind on earth will be bound in heaven, and whatever you loose in heaven will be loosed in earth."[3] Much focus is given to the "binding and loosing" when this scripture text is referred to or preached. I am convinced that the most important and overlooked part of the passage is, "and I will give you the keys to the kingdom of heaven." I have often said there is nothing wrong with Jesus, and the devil is not at war with Jesus. The war is between the devil and the church. You see, the devil is not omniscient, all knowing. He is not omnipresent, able to be everywhere at all times. He is surely not omnipotent, all powerful. He is a created being and the creature is not greater than the creator. He is not God's equal, He is God's opposite.

Many times people try to blame God for the war that Satan seems to be winning. I hear people say, "Well, if God is so strong why is all this evil prevailing? Why does the devil seem so strong?" The answer is both simple and complex. God is not in a battle, a war with the devil. If He was, this thing would have been over a long time ago. This battle is between the devil and the church. That's why Paul alerted the church in Ephesians 6 that what we are up against is not a battle between men. We don't wrestle with flesh and blood; our battle is against spiritual wickedness. It is against the powers of the air. It is against Satan and his demonic forces. The battle is not between God and the devil, nor Jesus and the devil. Jesus already defeated him at Calvary. The war is already won but the battle still rages. Jesus said in spite of the battle He would build His church and the gates of Hades would not prevail against it. We can be confident that the battle being waged by the devil will not prevail against the church.

THE BATTLE BEING WAGED BY THE DEVIL WILL NOT PREVAIL AGAINST THE CHURCH.

With all that said, we must understand *how* Jesus said we would prevail. He told us what He told the disciples on that day. He promised that He would give them (and us) some keys to the kingdom, and these keys are so powerful that whatever we bind on earth will be bound in heaven and whatever we loose on earth would be loosed in heaven. In other words, He was saying that when we use the keys He gives us, we will win every time. In Matthew 11:12 it says, "And from the days of John the Baptist until now the kingdom of heaven suffereth violence, and the violent take it by force."[4] Since the fall of man, people have been trying to force their way into the kingdom. Men have been trying to get His kingdom to come and His will to be done in the earth. But, Jesus promised to make available keys that would take away the need to seek to force our way into this kingdom authority. And He gives us keys and when we use them we will win every time.

Let me illustrate it this way. My wife and I were in Atlanta, Georgia for a conference hosted by a friend of mine. When traveling we always require a king size bed if we plan on sleeping well and have enough space. It so happened when we initially checked in only rooms with double beds were available. They told us to check back in a couple of days to see if any rooms with king beds had become available. By the grace of God, they had. Not only did we get a king room but we landed in a suite. The next morning we went down to the work out facility. When I came back to the room about an hour later, I went to use my key and the door wouldn't unlock. Needless to say these were the makings for a fleshy moment. Here I am standing out in the hallway, dripping wet with sweat, stinking up the hallway, and my key would not open the door. Already irritated, I prepared to go down to the front desk and rip into the management. Then I looked more closely at the key and I realized I still had the key to my first room. I was trying the open the door to my new room with the key to the old room. The key I was using was illegitimate.

Therein lies the problem with the church and the reason we find ourselves so often being defeated instead of defeating the kingdom of darkness. We're in the right kingdom with the right King, trying to open the right doors with the wrong keys. We are trying to get His will done in the earth, but the problem is we are using illegitimate keys. What we will find is this: if we will use the right keys, the kingdom of heaven will back us up. In other words, whatever we call into this earth when we use His keys, He will drop it out of heaven. The issue of racism is a spiritual problem. This is a spiritual battle for which God has a key. One of the keys most of the kingdom of God has not accessed is found in Psalm 133 where we find these words:

"Behold, how good and how pleasant it is for brethren to dwell together in unity! It is like the precious ointment upon the head, that ran upon the beard even Aaron's beard; that went down to the skirts. As the dew of Hermon, and as the dew that descendeth upon the mountains of Zion: for there the Lord commanded the blessing, even life forevermore."[5]

Blessing is the Hebrew word *"brakhah"* which means "benediction, benefit, peace." It also means, "favor." Favor means, "advantage, a condition conducive to success."[6] Jesus said when we use the keys to the kingdom which He gives us, we will have favor. We will have the advantage. We will win every time. If the church of Jesus Christ was to be honest, we would have to say there are times when we have not used all the keys He has made available to us. One of those keys is called unity! In fact, I believe it is the most important of all the keys God has given us. For the psalmist declared that where the brethren walk together in unity, there God commands the blessing. And that blessing is life forever more.

Life in the Hebrew is *"chay"* which translates to "vitality."[7] Another word for vitality is "dynamism" which comes from the root word "dynamite."[8] Dynamite, when taken in the context and reference of human beings, refers to a person possessing within them something extremely powerful. Now, put it all together and the psalmist said it is a wonderful thing when brethren dwell together in unity. Where brethren dwell in unity God commands the blessing. He commands His favor. That favor releases life, but not just any kind of life. That blessing releases the life filled with vitality; the life filled with dynamism, the life that releases the power of God in that atmosphere.

I am convinced this issue is the major key that God has given to His church. But we have failed to operate in its power because for the most part, we have not walked together in unity. Racist attitudes in many churches in America have caused us to remain divided, dysfunctional and delayed from our destiny. For though we have come a mighty long way, Dr. King's words ring true: "Eleven o'clock on Sunday morning is still the most segregated hour and a half of the week."

My first real experience with racism came as I was preparing for the ministry at one of our greatest Assemblies of God schools, Central Bible College in Springfield, Missouri. My experience on campus was wonderful thanks to a great president, Rev. Maurice Lednecky and his wife, Marcia. My experiences off campus, however, were a totally different story. It was required that we attend one of the many Assemblies of God churches in the Springfield area for Sunday services. To go anywhere else would require special permission. Being raised in the Church of God in Christ I didn't foresee this as a challenge since both were Pentecostal fellowships. My wife and I found out quickly what we had in common meant far less than what our difference was. I say difference because the only glaring difference I see is that the Assemblies of God is a predominantly white organization and the Church of God in Christ is predominantly black. We found out early this difference meant a lot more to many in the churches we sought to attend than the fact that we too were Pentecostal.

We had been told about how great one of the larger churches in the area was, so one Sunday morning we arose with great anticipation of enjoying our first worship service there. We drove up, jumped out of the car and joined nearly 2,500 others who had come to worship. When we walked through the door there was an elderly man smiling heartily and greeting people so warmly. That is, until it came time to greet my wife and me. When he turned around after greeting another couple, at the sight of us he suddenly took a step back, frowned, turned in the opposite direction and proceeded to greet someone else. Once we had cleared his view, he once again faced our direction and readily greeted others. That week I called the pastor to explain what had happened. The secretary was instructed to take a message and we were told someone would be calling us. Though I called more than once, that return phone call never came.

We were determined not to allow the enemy to get a foothold. We went to no less than six churches and received similar treatments. Finally, we found a church called Praise Assembly of God. The pastor was wonderful and for the most part we felt welcome. But one Sunday something happened that speaks to the heart of the issue in the kingdom of God. There was another black couple in that congregation. One Sunday the pastor asked everyone in the congregation who had ever invited someone black to their home, or gone out to dinner with someone black, to please stand. Only one couple in that congregation of over 600 people could stand. That was in the 1980s. I thought for sure we had moved to the place where at least in the kingdom of God we understood the power of Psalm 133. I am saddened to say that 33 years later not much has changed in the church of Jesus Christ.

I am convinced that Psalm 133 is the life and power of the church. I am convinced in my soul that the fullness of the realization of the words of Jesus in Matthew 16 hinges upon this Psalm 133 "key." This passage is the only scripture I find which declares that God commands blessing. Blessing in the Hebrew is *"tsawah,"* meaning "He decrees that His people will be victorious." It means that He ordains, establishes, and orders by superior authority that there is no way we can lose. You take the key of love and unity, you turn the thing, and whatever you bind on earth will be bound in heaven. Whatever you loose on earth will be loosed in heaven. If there is anywhere that the church has failed, I'm talking about the church universal, it is in the area of unity. In no other area have we been more divided than when it comes to the issue of race. It is the sin that very few preachers will call what it is, sin, and very few parishioners want to hear about. But as long as we ignore the issue, the church of Jesus Christ will remain divided, dysfunctional and delayed from our destiny.

We are the most powerful nation in the world, and I do not doubt that if we were wicked enough and desired to do so, we could wipe any nation off the face of the earth. But it is interesting to note that whenever the United States goes to war in a country, we do not target everything in that country. What is targeted is based on the strike potential. In other words, we strike only those things which have potential to harm us.

As the Body of Christ, we are in a war. We have been given command and authority to invade the kingdom of darkness. The devil applies the same war tactic to the kingdom of God. He targets Christians and ministries according to their "strike potential." That is, according to their ability to inflict damage to his kingdom of darkness. In I John 3:8b, John declared, "For this purpose was the Son of God manifested, that He might destroy the works of the devil."[9] John tells us that the main purpose in Jesus coming was to destroy or annihilate the destructive works of Satan. And Jesus said in Matthew 28:18-20 that now this is to be our purpose:

> *"All authority in heaven and on earth has been given to me. Therefore go and make disciples of all nations, baptizing them in the name of the Father and of the Son and of the Holy Spirit, and teaching them to obey everything I have commanded you. And surely I am with you always, to the very end of the age."[10]*

In Matthew 11:12 Jesus also said, "From the days of John the Baptist until now, the kingdom of heaven has been forcefully advancing, and forceful men lay hold of it."[11] In essence, Jesus was saying the whole purpose of His coming was to get the kingdom power of God in earth and to increase our strike potential. He was imploring us to take the authority we have been given and go make war against the devil's war.

I heard Pastor Rick Godwin say, "The devil doesn't care about us being saved as long as we don't become a target." I want to say that the devil doesn't care that a ministry exists, or that it is large as long as it doesn't become a target. He doesn't even put up his missile computer load zone if he does not consider you a target. In natural war and spiritual war, small or large, it is your strike potential that determines if indeed you are on the devil's radar as a threat which is worth giving attention to. That is why Satan fought so diligently, but unsuccessfully to take Jesus out. He understood the power of Jesus' strike potential. If you can't hurt the United States of America you are not a target. In this kingdom, if a ministry cannot hurt Satan's kingdom that ministry is not a target. There are many churches in America that are not targets of Satan, our enemy, because though they exist and may be large, they lack the potential to do damage to his kingdom.

There are a couple of reasons why Satan views many ministries as no threat to him. The first one is too many ministries are concerned about the things God is not concerned about and not concerned about the things God is concerned about. There are a lot of things that we focus on that are neither biblical nor kingdom advancing. There is a lot of majoring on minors in the kingdom of God. There is a lot of focus on the external rather than on the eternal.

WE FOCUS ON A LOT OF THINGS THAT ARE NEITHER BIBLICAL NOR KINGDOM ADVANCING.

I have been blessed to preach in a multitude of churches of different denominations and backgrounds. Sadly, what I have observed in many, regardless of denomination is they are so bound by legalism that blinds them to the real call of the kingdom. They are so concerned about making the rules and making sure that people don't break them, that they miss the most important thing in the kingdom … winning the lost to Christ. There are churches against so many things, I wonder if there is anything they are for. I recall preaching in one church where they were against women wearing earrings and makeup. To no avail, they put a full court press on my wife to remove both before the service started so that she would not "hinder" the anointing.

I am so thankful for the Pentecostal denomination in which I grew up, but I grew up in a church environment where it seemed that everything was a sin. Playing ball was a sin, men wearing shorts was a sin, women wearing pants was a sin ... and God knows if a woman wore makeup it was a sin. But no one needed to fret because she was surely going to hell where the heat would eventually melt it all away. Going to movies and playing Monopoly was a sin because the game had dice, and there must be demons hiding somewhere in those dice.

I share these examples not to make a mockery of my upbringing, nor to make fun of what some may yet believe today. Again, I am surely thankful for how I was raised and the church where I grew up. It was in that church I was taught something sorely missing in many church atmospheres today; a respect and reverence for a Holy God. But it is important to understand that those things people were against back then and some are against today are cultural beliefs and not biblical. This environment does not understand that the devil does not care if we major on minors. Just don't become a target! We are not a target to the enemy if we will not come against the things that really matter to God. One of those major things that keep the kingdom divided, dysfunctional and delayed from our destiny is racism. What I have found is that churches spend a lot of time fighting the wrong fight. And the devil simply laughs because as long as we fight the wrong fight and each other, we are not targets because we pose no danger to his dark kingdom.

RACISM—A SPIRIT OF WITCHCRAFT

At the beginning of this thesis I made the statement that ultimately racism is demonically driven. What I mean is that there is a demonic agenda behind the issue of racism. I know that this next statement

RACISM IS A SPIRITUAL PROBLEM | 69

may cause some to cringe, but I believe that racism is not only demonically driven, but it is driven by the spirit of witchcraft. In I Samuel 15:23 when confronting Saul's disobedience to God Samuel said to him, "For rebellion is as the sin of witchcraft; and stubbornness is as iniquity and idolatry."[12]

There are two definitions I want to draw from the word witchcraft. One applies to all people and the other, I believe, directly applies to Christians. Witchcraft is defined for us in this verse. It tells us that rebellion is compared to witchcraft, and a rebellious person is one who will not change their mind even when the Word of God says their way is wrong. A rebellious person is a stubborn person. Samuel also said that stubbornness is as iniquity and idolatry. Idolatry for the Christian is when a Christian makes a god out of their thoughts, no matter what God's Word says. Now all of this is important because we need to truly understand that what Samuel said to Saul on that day applies to all of us when we decide to go in a direction opposite of that which God has instructed.

There is a place for application of this scripture even in the area of racism. When a person claims to be a Christian, yet holds tightly to a separatist and racist mentality, that persons thinking is being governed by a spirit of witchcraft because that person is rebelling against the command of God. The Word of God declares in Galatians 3:28-29:

> "There is neither Jew nor Greek, there is neither slave nor free, there is neither male nor female; for ye are all one in Christ Jesus. And if ye be Christ's, then ye are Abraham's seed, and heirs according to the promise."[13]

And when anyone holds to a separatist spirit and claims that Jesus is the Lord of their life, they are in rebellion to the Word of God. And that is an influence of the spirit of witchcraft, pure and simple. John Bevere explains it this way:

> "The word witchcraft conjures up images of women in black reciting incantations, traveling by broom and scanning the future via a crystal ball while their cauldron simmers on the fire, or perhaps the more modern view is one who casts spells and curses upon others for influence or gain. Let's leave behind both concepts and discover the heart of witchcraft, no matter what form it takes ... obviously a true Christian would never practice witchcraft knowingly. But, how many today are under its influence because of the deception of rebellion?"[14]

Another definition of witchcraft is, "the control of other people or organizations through manipulation, intimidation or domination." Another word for witchcraft is divination. Divination is used often to control people by allegedly being able to forecast, or foretell the future."[15] Now please, do not shut down. Please, stay with the line of reasoning. Does this not show the picture of the greatest evil perpetrated on the black race in the history of earth. Slavery was driven by the desire of one group of people to manipulate, intimidate and dominate another group of people. And when anyone seeks to raise their ethnicity over another group, be sure the spirit of witchcraft is alive and well.

Samuel informed Saul that the spirit which gives power to witchcraft was the same one that was causing him to rebel against God. We must remember that in this kingdom, a rebellious and stubborn person is one who refuses to change direction even when the

Word of God says their way is wrong. In the Body of Christ, Jesus told us the right way to operate in the area of all relationships with all people, of all creeds, nations and colors. In Luke 10:27 He gave this instruction, "Love thy neighbor as thyself."[16] Yet in the church I pastor, and in churches all over America, there sit in our pews every Sunday people who are stubborn and rebellious toward this command, in spite of what the Word of God says.

And while no pastor can force anyone to obey the Word of God, we are required to preach and teach the truths of the Word of God. Pastors have the responsibility to compel those we lead to move toward the way in which God has commanded each of us to walk. I find in the area of racism many pastors never boldly address the issue. Pastors address a lot of other issues that we deem to be sinful … but not many are willing to address *this* issue and therefore, they are not a target. The devil doesn't really care too much that they deal with the other issues, as long as they don't deal with the issue of racism. Why? He understands that ultimately the church's success in reaching all people is found in unity. Nowhere is this more true than in the kingdom of God: as the leader goes, so go the people.

Pastors do not deal with the issue for one or more of three reasons: 1) Out of fear of the people; 2) not truly understanding the power of racism; or 3) not wanting to deal with their own issues concerning race. If pastors rebel against the Word of God when it comes to the issue of race, the people they pastor will follow their example. I am convinced that the church of Jesus Christ will never truly be able to raise the blood stained banner of Calvary and attack the forces of hell with full authority until we deal with the issue of racism that keeps us divided, dysfunctional and delayed from our destiny.

THE HOLY SPIRIT'S POWER TO BREAK RACISM

With all these observations, there is the other side of the coin. If racism is driven by the spirit of witchcraft, then the Holy Spirit is able to break that spirit. Romans 8:11-14 says:

> *"And if the same spirit of Him who raised Jesus from the dead is living in you, He who raised Christ from the dead will also give life to your mortal bodies through His spirit, who lives in you. Therefore, brothers, we have an obligation—but it is not to the sinful nature, to live according to it. For if you live according to the sinful nature, you will die, but if by the spirit you put to death the misdeeds of the body, you will live, because those who are led by the Spirit of God are the sons of God."* [17]

If we are claiming to be Christians, then this spirit not only applies to us, but works for us and in us as well. The same spirit that raised Christ from the dead works for us in order to work in us and through us what we cannot do in our own power. That same spirit of Christ living in each of us has the power to enable us to live a life that loves all people of every race, color and creed. It takes the work of the spirit to cause us to love some of those who are "like us." Therefore, it surely takes the work of the spirit to enable us to love those who are "not like us." And if the church of Jesus Christ is going to be used by God to break down walls of racism, we must understand that it is not a work that can be accomplished with the arm of the flesh. If we have the desire, God's got the power and enablement.

In John 14:28 Jesus told the disciples, "You heard me say, 'I am going away and I am coming back to you.'"[18] Notice, Jesus told His disciples some news that was initially hard for them to accept. For, they had forgotten very quickly what He told them moments earlier. In John 14:16 He gave them this promise, "I will pray to the Father. And He shall give you another comforter, that He may abide with you forever."[19] He was speaking of the Holy Spirit, the same spirit that raised Christ from the dead and now lives in His children.

Then in John 16:13, Jesus said this of the spirit, "But when He, the spirit of truth, comes, He will guide you into all truth."[20] Jesus made it very clear to His disciples that He did not come here to stay with them forever in the physical. But at the same time, He wanted them to understand that God had a greater plan that would allow Him to be with them and us always. That's why He told the disciples in Matthew 28:19, "Go ye therefore and make disciples of all nations ..."[21] He promised them He would be with them always. They didn't understand it all at the time and that promise was not fulfilled until after His resurrection. Jesus wanted them to understand that something greater was coming, that He would no longer "be with them" physically but "in them" spiritually. That was the promise of another counselor.

Max Lucado explains that there are two meanings for the word "another" in the Greek. One meaning refers to "something totally different." The other means, "another just like the first one."[23] This is important because the promise made to the disciples on that day remains in force for every subsequent disciple. Jesus told them not to worry about anything because the one He was sending would be as He was to them, everything they needed Him to be. He would be their comforter. He would be their shelter in the time of storm. He would give them peace in times of struggle. He would be exactly as Jesus was to them.

The difference now is that He lives in us in order to work through us. This is powerful because Jesus said of Him, the Holy Spirit, that He would lead and guide us into all truth. In that same verse, Jesus called Him "the spirit of truth."[23] So not only will He guide us into all truth, He will show us what truth is. But because He is truth, and He lives in us, He will enable us to live out the truth that He reveals. Therefore, once I come into the knowledge of the truth, I am also enabled by the spirit to live out that truth. What needs to be understood is that the issue of racism is a spiritual problem that, if the church will courageously and obediently confront, the Holy Spirit will enable us to reveal truth that will tear down walls of division which cause the Body of Christ to be divided, dysfunctional and delayed from our destiny.

There are those who have the attitude that racism is one of those issues that will always be with us. Because of this attitude, many think "why bother?" I submit that the sin is the issue that will be present for us to deal with until Christ returns. Sin has many avenues through which it flows, and racism is one of those avenues that must be dealt with until Christ returns.

E N D N O T E S

1. *NIV Study Bible (Red Letter Edition).* Edited by Kenneth Barker. Grand Rapids, Michigan: The Zondervan Corporation, 1985. Print.
2. Ibid.
3. Ibid.
4. *The Hebrew-Greek Key Study Bible (King James Version).* Edited By Spiros Zodhiates, Th.D. Chattanooga, Tennessee: AMG Publishers, 1984, 1991. Print.
5. Ibid.
6. Ibid.
7. Ibid.
8. *The American Heritage Dictionary. Second Edition.* Boston, Massachusetts: Houghton Mifflin Company, 1982, 1985. Print.
9. *The Hebrew-Greek Key Study Bible (King James Version).* Edited By Spiros Zodhiates, Th.D. Chattanooga, Tennessee: AMG Publishers, 1984, 1991. Print.
10. *NIV Study Bible (Red Letter Edition).* Edited by Kenneth Barker. Grand Rapids, Michigan: The Zondervan Corporation, 1985. Print.
11. *The Hebrew-Greek Key Study Bible (King James Version).* Edited By Spiros Zodhiates, Th.D. Chattanooga, Tennessee: AMG Publishers, 1984, 1991. Print.
12. Ibid.
13. Ibid.
14. Bevere, John. *The Devil's Door.* Orlando, FL: Creation House, 1996.
15. *The American Heritage Dictionary. Second Edition.* Boston, Massachusetts: Houghton Mifflin Company, 1982, 1985. Print.
16. *The Hebrew-Greek Key Study Bible (King James Version).* Edited By Spiros Zodhiates, Th.D. Chattanooga, Tennessee: AMG Publishers, 1984, 1991. Print.
17. *NIV Study Bible (Red Letter Edition).* Edited by Kenneth Barker. Grand Rapids, Michigan: The Zondervan Corporation, 1985. Print.
18. Ibid.
19. Edited by Rex Humbard Ministries. *Prophecy Bible Edition (The New King James Version).* Akron, Ohio: Thomas Nelson, Inc., 1985.
20. *NIV Study Bible (Red Letter Edition).* Edited by Kenneth Barker. Grand Rapids, Michigan: The Zondervan Corporation, 1985. Print.
21. Edited by Rex Humbard Ministries. *Prophecy Bible Edition (The New King James Version).* Akron, Ohio: Thomas Nelson, Inc., 1985.
22. Lucado, Max. *Fearless.* China: Hallmark/Thomas Nelson, Inc. Books, 2009.
23. *NIV Study Bible (Red Letter Edition).* Edited by Kenneth Barker. Grand Rapids, Michigan: The Zondervan Corporation, 1985. Print.

RACISM IS A SPIRITUAL PROBLEM.
THE HOLY SPIRIT WILL ENABLE US
TO REVEAL TRUTH THAT WILL TEAR
DOWN WALLS OF DIVISION WHICH
CAUSE THE BODY OF CHRIST TO
BE DIVIDED, DYSFUNCTIONAL AND
DELAYED FROM OUR DESTINY.

CHAPTER FOUR

GOD'S DEALINGS WITH RACISM
AN ISSUE THAT HAS BEEN AROUND SINCE THE FALL OF MAN

JONAH AND THE NINEVITES

Jonah was a prophet of God. God told Jonah to go down to Nineveh and preach to them about repenting. He told him to tell them that if they did not repent, He was going to destroy them. Jonah, who was Jewish, hated the Ninevites, who were Assyrians. He did not want to help them. "Instead of obeying God and going where he was instructed to go, he jumped on a boat and went to a place called Tarshish" (Jonah 1:3). Jonah was about to learn a difficult lesson in the area of rebellion. His reward for his disobedience is that God sends him a storm to get his attention. The storm is so strong that it will kill the innocent sailors. Jonah realizes that he is the cause of the storm and instructs them to throw him overboard. Once they do so, the storm ceases. Jonah gets swallowed up in the belly of a large fish. He remains in that fish for three days … which gave him plenty of time to repent.

Assyria is the area presently known as Iraq. Jonah hated the Assyrians and perhaps, rightfully so. The Assyrians were known as one of the most brutal nations of the ancient world. So brutal that they were feared and dreaded by the majority of the people of their day. History records they used the cruelest methods possible for torture and could easily extract information from captives. One of their favorite procedures was to take a man out onto the desert sands and bury him up to his neck with only his head remaining uncovered. They would then put a thong through his tongue and leave him in the hot sun to die. Imagine the heat beating down on their heads and poisonous critters like scorpions stinging them. It is said that a man would go mad before he died.[1] Some commentaries state that the Assyrians were so feared that when they moved on a town or village it was like a plague of locusts, causing entire towns to commit suicide rather than fall into the cruel hands of the Assyrians. These people were so brutal that in their surprise attacks, no one was spared. The women were taken captive and the men and children brutally slain.

When you consider the cruelty Jewish people faced at the hands of the Assyrians, it causes you to wonder what Jonah's experience may have been. The Bible doesn't give us an historical account of what Jonah may have personally witnessed or dealt with at the hands of the Assyrians. It could be a case of racism rooted in a negative personal experience as he saw them harm or kill people he cared about dearly. We don't know Jonah's personal experience, but we do know he hated the Assyrians and he did not want them saved. Couple Jonah's personal hatred with the overarching attitude shared by Israel that God had no concern for any other group outside of Israel, and it adds fuel to his fire. Simply put, because of his personal experience and popular belief among the Jews of superiority in the eyes of God, Jonah put all Assyrians in the same pot. In his mind there was no such thing as a good Assyrian—at least not good enough for him to risk crossing racial lines to try and save them.

MIRIAM, AARON AND MOSES' BLACK WIFE

In Numbers 12 we find Miriam and Aaron complaining behind Moses' back. In verses 1-2 we read these words:

"Then Miriam and Aaron spoke against Moses because of the Cushite (Ethiopian) whom he had married; for he had married a Cushite (Ethiopian) woman. And they said, 'Has the Lord indeed spoken only through Moses? Has He not spoken through us also?' And the Lord heard it."[2]

Most commentaries and people seem to believe that the real issue here was Miriam and Aaron's jealousy of Moses' authority, and the complaint about Moses' marriage to the Cushite woman was a smoke screen for their real issue. I believe it was actually the opposite. While I am sure they had some issue with submitting to Moses' leadership, I believe it only exposed a deeper and more hideous sin ... their racist spirits. The Bible very clearly states that Miriam and Aaron criticized Moses because they disagreed with his marriage to the Cushite woman. Being a Cushite meant that she was either Ethiopian or Sudanese, and the impression scripture gives us is that this was an issue for Miriam and Aaron from the beginning.

There is one thing I have learned about people, and we have all been guilty of this at some time or another. We will have a deep seeded issue with someone. It is brewing deep down inside, and we manage to keep it stuffed in there until suddenly something sets us off. We lose it and not only go after what just set us off, but also what is really the issue driving all the other issues. It comes flowing to the top like lava from a volcanic eruption. What I have found is that with most people, what they say is the issue is not really the issue. Rather, the issue they are blaming is covering up the main issue. It's interesting to me that God dealt with both issues. He dealt with the racism and the rebellion against Moses' authority. In Numbers 12:6 we read:

> "The He (God) said, 'Hear now my words: If there is a prophet among you, I, the Lord, make myself known to him in a vision, and I speak to him in a dream. Not so with my servant Moses; He is faithful in all my house. I speak with him face to face, even plainly, and not in dark sayings, and he sees the form of the Lord. Why then were you not afraid to speak against my servant Moses?'"[3]

God let them know they really didn't understand what kind of authority He had given to Moses. God asks them a very powerful question in vs. 8, "Why then were you not afraid to speak against my servant Moses?"[4] This is an interesting scripture in that Miriam and Aaron were mad at Moses because, in essence, he is messing up the family tree—bringing a black woman into this lighter skinned family. We need to comprehend the conversation occurring here. Though Aaron was seemingly as guilty as Miriam, God dealt directly with her. I have no answer as to why. Miriam could not simply admit that she was a racist at heart. She could not admit that she was mad at Moses for no other reason than him marrying this black woman. And she did what many people in the church do today; she cloaked her real issue with a spiritual robe.

In Numbers 12:2 she asked, "Doesn't God speak to others as well? Is Moses the only person that God speaks to?" We must not miss this very important point. She made her complaint sound spiritual. To the average listener, she sounded as one who was simply in a deeper pursuit of God. She sounded as one who desired to sincerely know if it is possible for God to speak to others the same way he speaks to Moses, for God is surely no respecter of persons. But, the truth was revealed in her questioning. The Bible very clearly states: "Miriam and Aaron began to talk against Moses because he had married a Cushite."[5] And in the church today, many times people use spiritual language to cover up what is really in their heart.

> **PEOPLE USE SPIRITUAL LANGUAGE TO COVER UP WHAT IS IN THEIR HEART.**

The Bible then tells us that as the cloud of God's glory moved away from the tent, the Lord's anger burned against them, and Miriam's skin suddenly became diseased … as white as snow! I am convinced that God was not only dealing with their evil and rebellious spirit, but also their spirit of racism. I picture in God's heart He is saying, "Okay, you don't like black, then I'll give you so much white you won't be able to stand it!" Please understand she was stricken with leprosy, or a similar disease. Miriam's disease became a condition that turned her skin milky white.[6] It was similar to that of a dead baby's skin. It suggests a variety of skin disorders from skin cancer or psoriasis to

Hansen's disease, which is the modern day designation for leprosy. I believe that God striking her flesh, her skin, was a sign that He was not going to tolerate their rebellion or their racist spirit of judging people by the color of their skin. I have heard the theory that in biblical times it was "spiritual" prejudice. I am convinced that it was the race issue He was dealing with on the front end. If it was simply and singly dealing with their rebellion, it seems to me that God would have touched her mouth rather than her skin.

PETER'S VISION

In Acts 10 there is the account of a centurion officer in the Roman army named Cornelius. He is a career officer with great influence. He was a member of what was known as the "Italian Band." The "Italian Band" was a group of Roman soldiers recruited in Italy. He had a reputation of being a "good man."[7] He was like many "good men" today, he lacked one thing … He was not a Christian. In his case, no one had yet delivered the Gospel to him. He had never heard of the Salvation of Jesus Christ. Yet there is one thing I find interesting about his account. Not only did he have a reputation for being a good man, he was also a praying man. He was a man who wanted to know God. My father often says that if a man calls out to God from the sincerity of his heart, God will come to him. The story of Cornelius is a testimony to that. Acts 10:3-6 gives this account:

> "At about three in the afternoon he (Cornelius) distinctly saw
> in a vision, an angel of God who came in and said, 'Cornelius!'
> Looking intently at Him, he became afraid and said, 'What is it
> Lord?' And He told him, 'Your prayers and your acts of charity

have come up as a memorial offering before God. Now send
men to Joppa and call for Simon, who is also named Peter. He
is lodging with Simon, a tanner, whose house is by the sea.'"[8]

So Cornelius does as God tells him. He sends these men to find
Peter. While they are on their way, God has to prepare Peter, for
Peter was going to have to deal with his racial issues. Again, we
have the issue and the reality that Jews of that day avoided all
contact with Gentiles. In other words, if you were not a Jew they
had nothing to do with you because in their minds, all others were
beneath them.

Scripture tells us that Peter goes up on the roof of this house to
pray. While he is up there he becomes overwhelmed with hunger,
but at the same time, he falls into a trance. He's not asleep. He's
having a vision. In the vision he sees a bed sheet coming out
of heaven. On the sheet are beasts, all kinds of birds, and bugs.
Verse 13 says that as he is seeing this strange vision, a voice said
to him, "Get up, Peter; kill and eat!"[9] Peter's response is interesting.
Understand, this instruction is coming from the Lord. Peter
responds by saying. "No Lord, for I have never eaten anything that
is common and unclean."[10]

I repeat, this instruction is not coming from a man. This
instruction is coming from the Lord himself! Peter is a man who
is living on the other side of Pentecost. He is a man who is living
in the dispensation of grace. He is a man who has witnessed the
power of God to set us free from the law. Yet, he is struggling to
break free of the law that was given under Moses. He is free from
the law, yet bound by the law. In seeking to keep the rigidity of the

rules of the law, he is blinded to the powerful thing God is seeking to do through him.

Jesus sets us free, yet we can remain bound! We are so willing to receive the blessings and grace of God, but struggle to give it to others. Jesus came to give us spiritual sight, yet, if we are not careful, we can remain blind. Such was the case of Peter. He is sincere, but sincerely wrong and misled.

Then in verse 15 the voice of God says to him, "'What God has made clean, you must not call common.' This happened three times, and then the object was taken up into heaven."[11] God tells Peter about the men coming and says, "Do not doubt that I have sent them." Peter is still dazed and confused. He is perplexed. Nevertheless, Peter goes with them to Cornelius' house. Cornelius sees them coming, runs up to Peter and falls down at his feet to worship him. In verse 26, Peter says to him, "Stand up, for I myself am just a man!"[12]

Next Peter informs Cornelius, "The reason you are falling down is because forever Jews thought that they were better than others."[13] Peter explains to Cornelius what he already knew: it was a law that Jews were not to keep company or come into the presence of one from another nation. Then Peter goes on to explain how God has opened his eyes and caused him to see that he should no longer call any man uncommon or unclean. In other words, the law says Jews and other ethnic groups are not supposed to have relationship, but when Jesus spoke into Peter's spirit and said not to call any man uncommon or unclean, it registered. Peter realized that he could no longer allow himself to be divided from those God loves because of their skin color, ethnicity or nationality. The message reads this way in Acts 10:27-29:

"You know I'm sure that this is highly irregular. Jews don't do this – visit and relax with people of another race. But God has just shown me that no race is better than any other. So the minute I was sent for, I came, no questions asked. But now I'd like to know why you sent for me." [14]

This account powerfully drives home how much the Father loves all mankind. This man, Cornelius, had been praying and fasting when God heard his prayer. This man doesn't even know Jesus as his personal savior, but he wanted to know him badly, to the point where he did what many Christians seldom do. He added fasting to his praying. But even more than Cornelius wanting to know God, God wanted Cornelius to know Jesus. That's why Jesus went to Calvary, was buried in the borrowed tomb of Joseph of Arimithea, and on the third day, God raised him from the dead. Immediately after the third day resurrection, Jesus said to Peter and the other disciples these words (Matthew 28:18-20):

"All authority has been given to me in heaven and on earth. Go therefore and make disciples of all the nations, baptizing them in the name of the Father and of the Son and of the Holy Spirit, teaching them to observe all things that I have commanded you; and lo, I am with you always, even to the end of the age. Amen." [15]

Go ye therefore and teach all nations. The word "nations" translates, "ethnicities of people." Jesus told them to go into the entire world, cross all racial barriers and tell them that He died for them. Tell them that He came to give them life more abundantly.

The reality is that Peter and the rest of the disciples received that command directly from the mouth of Jesus. Peter has been baptized in the Holy Spirit, with the evidence of speaking in tongues. Yet, it takes a vision from heaven to cause him to realize that he is not fulfilling the Great Commission. You can be a Christian, you can be Holy Ghost filled, fire baptized and that running over … you can speak in tongues, lay hands on the sick and they recover … God might have even allowed you to raise the dead, and you can *still* have issues to deal with that keep you from obeying the Great Commission.

Peter has been truly saved. He's not only been called to reach the lost, but has been given supernatural power by which to do so. Jesus said to them in Acts 1:8, "But you shall receive power when the Holy Spirit comes upon you; and you will be my witnesses in Jerusalem, and in all Judea and Samaria, and to the ends of the earth."[16] Peter has been anointed and appointed to preach this Gospel. Peter has all the power he needs. He is no longer living under the law, but by the spirit that lives in him.

Yet, he still had to come to grips with the reality that his racial issues, which were born out of what he had been taught, had to be dealt with if he was to truly obey the command of Jesus. This is the same Peter who, on the day of Pentecost declared (Acts 2:21), "And it shall come to pass, that whosoever shall call on the name of the Lord shall be saved."[17] What happened that day broke every racial barrier and brought the presence of God in such a powerful way that they had favor with all the people. Every day people were being added to the church by way of salvation. This is that same Peter. But, somewhere along the way he (and obviously all who were there that day) lost sight of God's agenda and that which was given to them to fulfill their assignment. Somehow they lost sight of the spiritual and began to once again focus on the physical. There is no doubt that Peter and those saved during that great outpouring of the spirit loved Jesus dearly, but still lost their way. We will look at this more deeply in chapter six. The same is true for us today. We can truly be saved and truly love Jesus while at the same time be used by the devil—if we do not deal with our race issues.

JESUS AND THE SAMARITAN WOMAN

This is one if my favorite stories in the Word of God, and one of the most powerful demonstrations of what can happen when we seek to address the issue of racism. In John 4 Jesus not only tells the disciples to cross ethnic and racial barriers, He shows them how. He goes to this Samaritan woman and requests a drink of water. We need to understand the depth and height of what is going on here. She is a Samaritan and Jesus is a Jew. Again we see the same pattern. The Jews of that day despised this ethnic group. If there was any group the Jews hated, it was the Samaritans. If they saw a Samaritan across the street and on fire, they wouldn't cross the street to pour a cup of water on them. But Jesus goes over to the Samaritan woman and asks her for a drink of water. He starts a conversation with her and she responds, "How is it that you, being a Jew, ask for a drink of me, a Samaritan woman? For Jews do not associate with Samaritans" (John 4:9).[18]

In our modern day language she would have said, "You do know who you are talking to, right? I mean, your people think they're too good to even have a conversation with us, never mind taking a drink from one of our wells." In love, Jesus answered (v. 10), "If you knew the gift of God, and who is saying to you, 'Give me a drink,' you would ask Him, and He would give you living water."[19] Jesus was telling her that she had no idea who was standing in front of her and what her future held because of His presence. She was not aware of whose presence she was standing in, but she was about to find out. If she knew, she would forget about the ethnic differences and ask Him for a drink instead of Him asking her.

As the conversation goes on she starts pointing out all the differences between her people and Jesus' people. Then she says (v. 19), "I see that you are a prophet."[20] Something supernatural takes place. The Samaritan woman begins to see that in spite of their ethnic differences, the hand of God is on this man who stands before her. But, it still doesn't quite connect for her. She reminds Jesus that the Jews claim that the place of worship is found in Jerusalem and the Samaritan's fathers worship on the very mountain on which they are standing. Then she informs Him that it never has been and it never shall be that Jews and Samaritans will come together in a worship service. She was letting Jesus know that she thinks He's a nice guy and has a sweet heart, but He needed to understand this ethnic barrier is never going to be broken. Jesus then made this powerful declaration vs. (21-24):

> *"Woman, believe me, the hour is coming when you will neither on this mountain, nor in Jerusalem worship the Father. You worship what you do not know; we know what we worship, for salvation is of the Jews. But the hour is coming, and now is, when the true worshipers will worship the Father in spirit and truth; for the Father is seeking such*

to worship him. God is spirit, and those who worship Him must worship in spirit and truth."[21]

Jesus declared to her that the true worshipers will worship in spirit and truth. He declared that there is coming a day when flesh won't be the issue, when flesh is going to get out of the way and the spirit will be the only thing that matters. Worship won't be measured by outward appearance and display. Something is going to happen in the spirits of men where worship becomes so real that flesh will not even enter the equation. Worship will be so real as to not be by might, nor by power, but by the spirit. Every barrier will come down and the true worshipers, those led by the spirit, whose spirit eyes are enlightened to the truth, will come together and worship. When that happens, color won't matter! Ethnicity won't matter! Social status won't matter! Financial status won't matter! Education won't matter! The poor man will worship next to the rich man! The man with the Harvard degree will worship next to the man with the G.E.D.! The man with the multi-wage will worship next to the man making the minimum wage!

Jesus made a declaration that the day was coming, and is already here for those who will see it, when the black man will link arms with the white man. The white man will link arms with the yellow man. The yellow man will link arms with the red man. The red man will link arms with the olive man, and none of this will happen by force. Jesus was informing the Samaritan woman that the day is coming when ethnic groups from every corner of this people planet will be able to worship together.

Now, when is this day? That day is not the same for everyone. That day comes when the flesh gets out of the way and our worship

is done in spirit and in truth. That day comes when we truly see Jesus. I believe that day is similar to what Isaiah experienced when he wrote these words (Isaiah 6:1-6):

> "In the year that King Uzziah died, I saw the Lord seated on a throne, high and exalted, and the train of his robe filled the temple. Above him were seraphs, each with six wings: with two wings they covered their faces, with two they covered their feet, and with two they were flying. And they were calling to one another: 'Holy, holy, holy is the Lord Almighty; the whole earth is full of His glory.' At the sound of their voices the doorposts and threshold shook and the temple was filled with smoke. 'Woe to me' I cried. 'I am ruined. For I am a man of unclean lips, and my eyes have seen the King, the Lord Almighty.' Then one of the seraphs flew to me with a live coal in his hand, which was taken with the tongs from the altar. With it he touched my mouth and said, 'See, this has touched your lips; your guilt is taken away and your sin atoned for.'"[22]

King Uzziah was dead and Isaiah was bummed out. He was wondering how they could go on, but he was wise enough to go to the house of God to worship the Lord. And in that worship experience, God's presence came and Isaiah got a true revelation of his own heart. True worship does that. True worship opens our eyes to who God is and what we need to be. When Isaiah came into true worship, his flesh died. When his

TRUE WORSHIP OPENS OUR EYES TO WHO GOD IS AND WHAT WE NEED TO BE.

flesh died he no longer operated and thought with the soul man—
the seat of his thought life, will and emotions. Instead he began
to listen to his spirit man. Jesus was speaking to the spirit of the
Samaritan woman, informing her that there is coming a day when
flesh will get out of the way and die, and it will be because of true
worship. Let's read John 4:21-23 from the Message Bible:

> "Believe me, woman, the time is coming when you
> Samaritans will worship the Father neither here at this
> mountain nor there in Jerusalem. You worship guessing in the
> dark; we Jews worship in the clear light of day. God's way of
> salvation is made available through the Jews."[23]

There are three very important issues from this passage:

1. Jesus stated that the Samaritan woman was accurate when
    she announced that her people worship where she said
    they worshiped. That was a fact.

2. Jesus made it clear to her that God was making a way for
    her to be saved through the very people who despised her.

3. Jesus made it clear that the time was coming, and in fact
    had already come, when what you are called and where
    you go to worship will not matter.

In other words, there is coming a day when it won't matter what
name is on the building. There is coming a day when where you
were born and the family tree you are connected with will not
matter, ethnicity will not matter. It will not matter what you are
called. Worship is not about being around people like you. Worship
is not about being around people who look like you. It's not about

being separated unto your own kind. The only kind that will matter is the kind who worships in spirit and truth. John 4:23 says:

> "It's who you are and the way you live that count before God. Your worship must engage your spirit in pursuit of the truth. That's the kind of people the Father is out looking for: those who are simply and honestly themselves before him in their worship. God is sheer being itself-spirit. Those who worship Him must do it out of their very being, their spirits, their true selves, in adoration."[24]

Here is where so many Christians struggle with the issue of race. We forget, or don't realize, that we are first spirit, then soul, and then body. The natural man operates in reverse. The natural man takes care of the body first, then his soul, and finally his spirit—if he ever gets around to the latter. Even Christians, unless we are taught and make the decision to put these in their proper order, continue to live in this kingdom as we did in the kingdom of which we came out of, the kingdom of the world. Though the kingdom of God is in us, we must make the soul man submit to the spirit man.

The disciples give us proof of what I have just stated. While Jesus is having this conversation with the Samaritan woman, the disciples go away to take care of other business. When they return and see Jesus talking to this woman, they are shocked. They can't believe Jesus is talking to "that" kind of woman. John 4:27 records:

> "Just then His disciples came back. They were shocked. They couldn't believe he was talking with that kind of woman. Only one said what they were 'all' thinking, but their faces showed it."[25]

That is just an ugly picture of a whole lot of people in the Body of Christ. They are saved … and still fleshy. They may even tolerate and go to church where there are different ethnicities. And they are not going to say it, but, their faces tell the story. To many of them it is easier to have a root canal than it is to accept all these "other" people in "our" church.

ENDNOTES

1. McGee, J. Vernon. *Through the Bible with J. Vernon McGee (Volume III Proverbs-Malachi)*. Nashville, Tennessee: Thomas Nelson, Inc., 1982..

2. Edited by Rex Humbard Ministries. *Prophecy Bible Edition (The New King James Version)*. Akron, Ohio: Thomas Nelson, Inc., 1985.

3. Ibid.

4. Ibid.

5. Ibid.

6. *The Apologetics Study Bible.* Edited by Ted Cabal. Nashville, Tennessee: Holman Bible Publishers, 2007. Print.

7. McGee, J. Vernon. *Through the Bible with J. Vernon McGee (Volume III Proverbs-Malachi)*. Nashville, Tennessee: Thomas Nelson, Inc., 1982.

8. *The Apologetics Study Bible.* Edited by Ted Cabal. Nashville, Tennessee: Holman Bible Publishers, 2007. Print.

9. Ibid.

10. Ibid.

11. Ibid.

12. Ibid.

13. Ibid.

14. *The Message (Numbered Edition).* Ed. Eugene H. Peterson. Colorado Springs, Colorado: Navpress, 2005. Print.

15. Edited by Rex Humbard Ministries. *Prophecy Bible Edition (The New King James Version)*. Akron, Ohio: Thomas Nelson, Inc., 1985.

16. *NIV Study Bible (Red Letter Edition).* Edited by Kenneth Barker. Grand Rapids, Michigan: The Zondervan Corporation, 1985. Print.

17. *The Hebrew-Greek Key Study Bible (King James Version).* Edited By Spiros Zodhiates, Th.D. Chattanooga, Tennessee: AMG Publishers, 1984, 1991. Print.

18. *The Apologetics Study Bible.* Edited by Ted Cabal. Nashville, Tennessee: Holman Bible Publishers, 2007. Print.

19. Ibid.

20. Ibid.

21. Edited by Rex Humbard Ministries. *Prophecy Bible Edition (The New King James Version).* Akron, Ohio: Thomas Nelson, Inc., 1985.

22. *NIV Study Bible (Red Letter Edition).* Edited by Kenneth Barker. Grand Rapids, Michigan: The Zondervan Corporation, 1985. Print

23. *The Message (Numbered Edition).* Ed. Eugene H. Peterson. Colorado Springs, Colorado: Navpress, 2005. Print.

24. *NIV Study Bible (Red Letter Edition).* Edited by Kenneth Barker. Grand Rapids, Michigan: The Zondervan Corporation, 1985. Print.

25. Ibid.

CHAPTER FIVE

RACISM IN THE CHURCH

EXAMPLES OF RACISM IN THE PRESENT DAY CHURCH

I am blessed to pastor a multi-cultural, multi-ethnic church. There are more than 50 nations represented in this precious church. You name them, and you can probably find them in our church. But I am wise enough to know having this diverse environment in our church does not mean that there are not those who battle with race issues. A case in point is when a wonderful woman of God in our church came to see my wife and me. She is of African descent and somewhere in the conversation her nephew's recent marriage to a beautiful Caucasian woman came up. Suddenly her whole demeanor changed, her voice dropped and she said, "Pastor, you probably noticed that I wasn't at the wedding." I replied, "Yes, I did." She proceeded to explain to us, "The reason I wasn't there was because he married that white girl." That meeting suddenly became short as she saw the stunned look on our faces. She knows that in Eagle Heights Church if we find racism trying to rear its ugly head, we will not tolerate it.

My point is that this woman worships in the same church as other ethnicities. She ushers in this church filled with people who are not "like" her. She even attends many of the church events with people of different ethnic backgrounds. She has heard me preach on this issue on more than a few occasions as well as seeing me confront the issue. Yet, when someone of a different ethnic background crossed "the line," the true condition if her heart was revealed.

The Body of Christ must learn that you don't choose a church because everybody looks like you, walks and talks like you. You choose a church because the Spirit of the Lord is there, and there is liberty. You don't just tolerate people—you allow the Holy Spirit to love through you. 2 Corinthians 3:17 says, "Now the Lord is that Spirit; and where the Spirit of the Lord is, there is liberty."[1] Liberty: "free to be me." No matter the color of my skin or the texture of my hair. In the church where the Spirit of the Lord is, and the people worship in spirit and in truth, every person is free to be whoever and whatever God made them to be.

I remember Pastor Casey Treat sharing about the time when a young man walked up to him on a Sunday after service. The young man had been attending church for a few weeks. He's a black man and seemed to be enjoying the services. That day he approached Pastor Treat and said, "Pastor, I love your church. I love the people. I love the preaching. But, I can't come here anymore." Casey Treat asked, "Why?" The man answered, "Because all my black friends keep telling me you ought to not be going over there to that white man's church." Casey looked at him and responded saying, "You mean to tell me in this time we live in, you're gonna let some racist people cheat you out of the anointing and the blessing of God?"

Several years ago, I heard Pastor Rick Godwin preach a message by the title, "'A' Level Christianity." Rick pastors a multi-cultural church and in the message he tells of a woman named Sandra Steen who attends his church. Sandra came there from an all black church. She came to his church and great pressure was put on her. Her former pastor said to her, "Sandra, you need to be loyal to the brothers. You shouldn't be over there in that white man's church!" I love Sandra's response. She said, "Pastor, I love you, but black dead is just as dead as white dead." Rick Godwin said, "You don't choose a preacher by the color. You choose one by the anointing."

Jesus said there is coming a day, and it is already here, where true worshipers will worship in spirit and in truth. Christians have got to learn that you don't choose a church by the color of a man's skin. You choose a church by the anointing upon the house. To break the demon spirit of racism we have got to be willing to take a stand in spite of criticism.

TO BREAK THE DEMON SPIRIT OF RACISM WE HAVE GOT TO BE WILLING TO TAKE A STAND IN SPITE OF CRITICISM.

When I became the pastor of Eagle Heights Church I followed an Italian pastor who had passed away a few years prior. We changed the name from Parkway Christian Center to Eagle Heights Church, but we were very cautious. We did not want to make too many changes too fast in order for people to adjust to my leadership style. Most of the board members I inherited were Italian, Irish or Polish. One of the Irish board members called me shortly after I moved into my office and asked to take me out to lunch. It seemed that he was adjusting well to my leadership style. We were having a wonderful conversation when he switched directions suddenly. He felt bad about informing me that he and his family were going to be leaving the church. I asked him if it was because he was having difficulty adjusting to my leadership style. He assured me that was not the case, and that his teenage children loved my style of preaching. Then the truth finally came out. He informed me that his wife was uncomfortable worshiping with so many minorities. Now here is the most interesting part: supposedly she had no problem with her pastor being black, but she was uncomfortable with so many Puerto Rican and Africans starting to attend the church. I thought, "How sad that in this day and age in church, where people claim the deep infilling of the Holy Spirit, so much of our thinking is dictated by our flesh."

On the other side of the coin, a beautiful Hispanic family came to me one day and said, "Pastor, we're coming to this church. But we want you to know that we've been told we shouldn't be here, instead we ought to be attending a Hispanic church." The father then said to me, "But, we didn't pick our church for the culture. We picked it for the anointing! We chose it because of the presence of God." To live, write about and teach this message means sacrifice for both pastors and the people they lead. But as we will discuss in the next few chapters, the church has a call and mandate where the issue of racism is concerned, no matter the cost.

THE MODERN CHURCH'S STANCE ON RACISM

He was born in Austria on April 20, 1889. No one could have known how this little baby would one day grow up to become one of Satan's most anointed tools of hatred and racism. It is said that though he was a very bright student, Adolf Hitler was also a lazy student who never graduated from high school. Yet, this demented man would rise to great military and political power. His march toward control began in 1919, but it was not just a campaign for control. It was a campaign rooted in a deep seeded hatred, fueled by a desire to destroy the Jews. It is the same agenda that Satan has had down through history. This little man's hatred of the Jews was verbalized in rhetoric that revealed the very nature of his heart. It is said that he referred to the Jews as, "The personification of the devil, the symbol of all evil." He said by defending myself against the Jews, I am doing the work of the Lord."[2]

David Adler shares that in 1933, Adolf Hitler came into power and the assault began as he declared that the German people were the "… founders of culture … a master race, superior to all other groups, superior to blacks, gypsies, poles, Jehovah's Witnesses, homosexuals, and especially the Jews!"[3] Under Hitler, prejudice and discrimination became public policy. Adler shares many testimonies of Jewish people who survived Hitler's assault including this one from a man named Ernist Honig:

> "It was early evening when the rain stopped and the doors opened. As I came off the train, I saw on the left huge chimneys belching forth thick black smoke. There was a strange smell, like the burning feathers off a chicken before it was cooked."[4]

At that time, he didn't know that the smoke and the smell were not from chickens. What he smelled was their own flesh, their own families burning. They were smelling victims of Hitler's demonic plan unfolding. Story after story has been told to demonstrate how demonic not only Hitler's hatred was, but how demonic hatred is. For centuries, in times of trouble Jews have been convenient scapegoats. They have been wrongly blamed for wars, poverty, plagues, diseases and anything else which is wrong in the world. But what is most troublesome about Hitler's hatred is that history records that even some church leaders spoke out against the Jewish people in Hitler's favor.[5]

I shared that account in order to accentuate this reality: history tells us in many cases, the church of Jesus Christ has stood on the wrong side of the issue of racism. There have been those who have blatantly embraced racism in the church. Then there are those who have passively accepted it, hiding behind the theory of "homogenous churches" working better than having churches with racial and ethnic diversity. If you don't know what that means, simply put, it is the belief that you can only build strong and successful churches of those who are alike.

HISTORY TELLS US IN MANY CASES, THE CHURCH HAS STOOD ON THE WRONG SIDE OF THE ISSUE OF RACISM.

Still, others are firmly against racism, but have the attitude that is much like that which I call the "ostrich mentality," where we stick our heads in the sand as though we cannot see nor be seen and not understanding that our big ole bodacious rear-end is still sticking out. The thinking that believes that if we just ignore it, we will see no evil and evil will not touch us. I submit the church above all others should not ignore the reality that racism is alive and well and we have been the ostrich in this case. We have built our large and fancy buildings. We produce our wonderful Christmas and Easter pageants. We hold large revivals with some of the biggest names in the catalog of preachers. We have some of the greatest children and youth ministries in many of our churches today. And I am not against any of these things. But largely, we have not only tolerated, but have ignored the responsibility the church has to deal with this sin called "racism" while doing big things. Indeed, we have for the most part, stuck our head in the sand to avoid dealing with racism. Thus, we have not functioned well in our number one job description. In Matthew 28:18-20 Jesus gave the disciples and all subsequent disciples this job description:

> He said, "All authority has been given to me in heaven and on earth. Go, therefore, and make disciples of all nations, baptizing them in the name of the Father and of the Son and of the Holy Spirit, teaching them to observe everything I have commanded you. And remember, I am with you always, to the end of the age."[6]

In those two verses lies the flesh and bones of the job description for every Christian. Jesus said, "Go ye therefore and teach all nations." Nation means *"ethe"* which is the root word for "ethnic" or "ethnicities." Jesus told his disciples of yesterday and today, the number one priority of our job description is to cross all racial barriers. We are to cross all ethnic barriers and tell them that He loves them and that He came to let them know by dying for them. We are to let them know that it was not just for certain people, but for all people. We have been commanded to cross every ethnic barrier and tell them that Jesus loves them.

What the church must do is realize that we have a call, not to be a giant organization, but to be an organism that is alive with the power of God and performing the will of God. The will of God is found in 2 Peter 3:9, "… not willing that any should perish but that all should come to repentance." We must recognize that we are the answer to every social ill that plagues humanity. Neither the government nor the White House is the answer to the world's ills. These entities can aid and assist, but they are not and do not have the answer to the spirit of racism that plagues this nation. Time has allowed us to observe that what the government mostly does is deal with the symptoms, not the sickness, and many times it does not do that well. Poverty is a symptom of a sickness. Murder is a symptom of a sickness. Abortion is a symptom of a sickness. Spousal and sexual abuse are symptoms of a sickness. In a world that seems to label everything as a sickness we need to understand that alcoholism and drug addiction are not sicknesses per say. They are symptoms of a sickness. The statistics of alcoholism and drug addiction are staggering, but all of these unbelievable issues are the symptoms not the sickness.

The government tries to fix things and I applaud the effort, but all they are touching are the symptoms. Racism is a symptom of a great sickness that very few preachers even preach about anymore in this seeker sensitive day of the church. It's called "sin!" Sin is the sickness! Sin is the disease and every human being is born with it! It does not matter how excellent your gene pool is. It doesn't matter if your family tree is so healthy your loved ones live to be 100 years of age, sleeping their way into glory. It does not matter because there is one disease that does not discriminate. The cure, the medicine for all sin, still remains the same as it was 2,000 years ago. His name is Jesus. Racism is a disease that can only be cured by this medicine.

Racism isn't a political problem or agenda that government policies can solve, but it is unequivocally a spiritual issue that can only truly be addressed by a church that desires to honor Christ! Racism has been exploited by both political parties when convenient, but the church must understand that racism is first and foremost a sin to be confronted by those who seek to live out the call to a reconciliatory lifestyle.

ENDNOTES

1. *The Hebrew-Greek Key Study Bible (King James Version)*. Edited By Spiros Zodhiates, Th.D. Chattanooga, Tennessee: AMG Publishers, 1984, 1991. Print.
2. Adler, David A. *We Remember the Holocaust*. New York, New York: Scholastic, Inc., 1989.
3. Ibid.
4. Ibid.
5. Ibid.
6. *The Apologetics Study Bible*. Edited by Ted Cabal. Nashville, Tennessee: Holman Bible Publishers, 2007. Print.

RACISM IS A SYMPTOM OF A GREAT SICKNESS CALLED SIN. SIN IS THE DISEASE AND EVERY HUMAN BEING IS BORN WITH IT! THE ONLY CURE IS JESUS.

CHAPTER SIX

THE CALL

STAND IN THE GAP—BUILD UP THE WALL

I am convinced in my spirit that there is a call to the 21st century church from the throne room of God—the church must no longer keep silent on the issue of racism. This call rings louder than ever in Ezekiel 22:29-31:

> "The people of the land practice extortion and commit robbery; they oppress the poor and needy and mistreat the alien, denying justice. I looked for a man among them who would build up the wall and stand in the gap on behalf of the land so that I would not destroy it, but I found no one. So I will pour out my wrath on them and consume them with my fiery anger, bringing down on their heads all they have done, declares the Sovereign Lord."[1]

Hear the words of the Lord: stand in the gap … build up the wall! God is saying today what He said in Ezekiel's day. He is looking for someone who will boldly stand up, who will keep silent no more, who will speak the truth in love, power and authority. History shows that whenever the body of Christ was silent and did not lift its voice against injustice, the powers of hell were most successful and progressive.

Whenever the church has said anything, it has usually been some preacher pounding a podium in anger over what wrongs have been perpetuated against his people and who perpetuated them. There has been a lot of name calling, but few answers. Then there is the other side of the coin. There are others who have said that we don't need to go overboard with this issue of racism because they feel we have made such great progress. In the area where I live, there are those in the church world who hold this attitude. Because we have somehow managed to get a few thousand people together once a year for Boston Night of Worship (and I applaud those who have this vision) that we do not have a race problem. We are at best remiss, and at worst ignorant, if we believe that having a worship gathering once or twice a year (where we sing songs in Spanish or Portuguese and English and have leaders of various ethnicities constitutes a declaration), that racism is no longer an issue in the Body of Christ.

If we believe church gatherings of different races in any way negates the reality of racism, not only in the world but in the church as well, we are severely confused, misled and deceived. Many people leave such gatherings on Sunday and go back to work on Monday with the same racial attitudes they embraced on Saturday before the Sunday worship service. Even if we don't promote racist attitudes, we aid them in their existence because we tolerate them in those around us, both in the saved and unsaved alike. I for one believe that while everything that is wrong in the world is not the church's fault, it is our responsibility to answer the call, to stand in the gap and uproot unrighteousness wherever we see it and in whatever form it takes. God has not only given us the call, He has defined it for us.

THE CALL DEFINED—THE MINISTRY OF RECONCILIATION

In Romans 5:10-11, Paul says:

> *"For if, when we were enemies, we were reconciled to God by the death of His son, much more, being reconciled, we shall be saved by His life. And not only so, but we also joy in God through our Lord Jesus Christ, by whom we have received the atonement."*[2]

Reconciliation is the act of settling a dispute between two parties and restoring them back into friendly relationship.[3] This is what Paul is telling the Romans: while we were enemies of God, while God had rightful dispute with sinful men and women, He reconciled us, and brought us back into right relationship with Him. He did it through the death of His son. How awesome it is when we recognize that we who were once enemies of God are now friends of God. Then He lets us know that with reconciliation come responsibility. In 2 Corinthians 5:18-21, Paul wrote:

"And all things are of God, who hath reconciled us to Himself by Jesus Christ, and hath given to us the ministry of reconciliation; to wit, that God was in Christ, reconciling the world unto Himself, not imputing their trespasses unto them; and hath committed unto us the word of reconciliation. Now then we are ambassadors for Christ, as though God did beseech you by us; we pray you in Christ's stead, be reconciled to God. For He hath made Him to be sin for us, who knew no sin; that we might be made the righteousness of God in Him."[4]

Let's look at two key words in this passage. The first is reconciliation, which as stated means to "reestablish friendship between; to settle or resolve as a dispute." The other is the word "ambassadors" which means, "an authorized representative with an official message."[5]

The first thing we must grasp is the apostle Paul saying Jesus came and reestablished our relationship with God. The truth is that God had a rightful dispute with mankind. The first man, Adam, rebelled against God and man has been rebelling against God ever since. We were on our way to a devil's hell because God's righteousness would not allow Him to tolerate man's sin. In order to settle that dispute, there needed to be reconciliation. Jesus was beaten, spat on, nailed to a wooden beam, and blood flowed from His battered and beaten body as a sword was rammed through His side. The blood flowed like a river, but with it came the washing away of man's sin. They buried Him in the borrowed grave of Joseph of Arimithea. But, on the third day, God raised Him from the dead. With that resurrection, not only were our sins' stains removed, but we were reconciled back to God. All who repent and call Him Savior receive the gift of reconciliation. Romans 3:23-25 declares this powerful and wonderful truth:

"For all have sinned, and fallen short of the glory of God; and are justified freely by His grace through the redemption that come by Christ Jesus: God presented Him as a sacrifice of atonement, through faith in His blood. He did this to demonstrate His justice, because in His forbearance, He had left the sins committed beforehand unpunished ..."[6]

There is a song we sang years ago that spoke to this truth. It said, "What can wash away my sin? Nothing but the blood of Jesus." From that day forward the dispute was resolved and the opportunity for reconciliation became available for all mankind, without regard of race, color or ethnicity.

But there is something many do not realize or recognize. When reconciliation came to man, responsibility also came to man. Paul informed us in 2 Corinthians 5:18-21 that when we receive the blessing of reconciliation, we become responsible for the ministry of reconciliation.[7] He tells us that when we take part in the born-again experience we become Christ's ambassadors. And as His ambassadors He committed to us the Word, or the responsibility of the ministry of reconciliation. Not only do we have the responsibility, we also have the authority. Remember, an ambassador is "an authorized representative with an official message." He gave to us the responsibility and the authority to carry to the world the official message of heaven. What is this message? It is found in John 3:16:

"For God so loved the world that He gave His only begotten son, that whosoever believes in Him should not perish, but have everlasting life."[8]

And John 10:10:

> *"The thief cometh not, but for to steal, and to kill, and to destroy: I am come that they might have life, and that they might have it more abundantly."*[9]

That's the official message of the ministry of reconciliation. It is the message that declares this is not a white gospel, or a black gospel, or a red gospel, or a yellow gospel. This is a "whosoever will, may come" gospel. He didn't authorize the government to deliver this message. He didn't authorize the White House to deliver this message. Neither are these entities responsible for this message. The only entity responsible for and authorized to carry this message is the church of Jesus Christ. It's an official message not authorized and signed with presidential ink, but with the Holy Ghost anointed finger of Jesus who said, "Go ye therefore and teach all nations."[10] He told us to deliver this official message to all nations.

This is a difficult assignment if we do not fully understand what Paul was saying. Here is a clearer picture of what Paul is trying to get across (2 Corinthians 5:18-21):

> *"Now we look inside, and what we see is that anyone united with the Messiah gets a fresh start, is created new. The old life is gone; a new life burgeons! Look at it! All this comes from the God who settled the relationship between us and Him, and then called us to settle our relationships with each other. God put the world square with Himself through the Messiah, giving the world a fresh start by offering forgiveness of sins. God has given us the task of telling everyone what He is doing. We're*

Christ's representatives. God uses us to persuade men and women to drop their differences and enter into God's work of making things right between them. We're speaking for Christ Himself now: Become friends with God; He's already a friend with you."[11]

I hope you see it! Paul is telling us that we, as God's ambassadors, are speaking for Him to let the world know that their sins can be forgiven—that a man can have a fresh, new start in life. He tells us that once we give our lives to God, He wants to use us to tell mankind about the wonderful gift of salvation that has been provided for them. If we are going to do this, we have got to get rid of those things that separate us and stand between us. Thus, keeping us from being the ministers of reconciliation, the ambassadors He needs us to be. Racism is one of the greatest weapons Satan uses in order to keep the church of Jesus Christ separated.

SATAN USES RACISM TO KEEP THE CHURCH OF JESUS CHRIST SEPARATED.

In many Christian churches today we have yet to understand the full meaning of the words in Galatians 3:28 where it says, "There is neither Jew nor Greek, there is neither bond nor free, there is neither male nor female; for ye are all one in Christ Jesus."[12] I do not think it is a stretch or heresy if I were to say this scripture could also read like this to the 21st century church: "There is neither black nor white, there is neither Puerto Rican nor Italian, there is neither Irish nor Portuguese, Mexican nor Native American, Asian nor Jew." Or, it could be read, "There is neither Baptist nor Methodist, there is neither Assemblies of God nor Church of God in Christ. There is neither Pentecostal nor Charismatic, nor

Independent ..." In the biblical kingdom of God there is no division. Paul gives this admonition in Romans 16:17: "Now I beseech you, brethren, mark them which cause divisions and offenses contrary to the doctrine which ye have learned; and avoid them."[13] Paul tells us to avoid those who are the cause of divisions. Yet, for fear of loss of money or membership, pastors will put up with racists attitudes in their churches that divide the Body of Christ.

One of the major reasons racism is alive in the one place it should not be—churches in America—is because most white brethren don't want to talk about it, and many black brethren want nothing else but to talk about it. If we are going to be biblical churches we must be ambassadors of reconciliation, first in the church, then outside the church. The problem in many cases is that our message is watered down because we are trying to bring something to the world that much of the church has not yet experienced. We are trying to bring the love of Christ to the world without fully embracing its message first in the church.

If we are going to bring a message of hope to the world, we must first be willing to acknowledge that there have been hurts in the past from all sides of the racial groups in this nation. We have got to repent and forgive one another so that we can truly begin to live out Dr. King's dream, so we can truly live in a nation where one is judged by the content of one's character rather than by the color of one's skin. We must realize that this type of judgment doesn't only go on outside church walls, but in the very confines of the church walls as well. The Body of Christ would do well to ask ourselves individually and corporately the words of the song sung by Billy Ocean, "What is the color of love ... what do you see?"[14]

When we judge people by the color of their skin, our expectation of them is tainted as well. The October 18, 2012 *Miami Herald* ran an article titled, "Criticism Follows Florida's Race Based Student Achievement Goals." It stated that when the state grades its teachers, there is no accounting for student's race or economic status. But, when Florida sets academic performance goals it will grade itself on a curve with targets related to race, income, disability and English proficiency. For example, Florida hopes to have 86% of white students at or above grade level math, but for blacks the goal is 74%."[15] I understand that some groups come in with fewer advantages than others. It is common knowledge that some come from less advantageous situations due to poor family structure. But, here's what I struggle with: the color of a person's skin is not the issue. The environment in which they have to seek to thrive in is the issue. It's amazing to me how so many decisions are made because of the color of skin—not only in the world, but in the church as well.

I spoke at an event attended mainly by Caucasians. I will never forget what one woman said to me afterwards. She walked up to me and without skipping a beat said, "I wasn't going to come because I heard the speaker was a black man. But I'm so glad I came because you don't sound black. You speak so clearly. You exceeded my expectations."

Former NBA great, Charles Barkley, tells the story from years ago while sitting in the first class section of a train. A fellow passenger, not knowing who he was, walked up to him and said, "You're sitting in the first class section." The implication was that because of the color of his skin he obviously didn't belong in such a place. I have been in churches that have given me the same impression.

Again, I want to emphasize that racism is not a black and white issue. Racism is a people issue.

A few years back I had a young man on staff who served as my youth pastor. He was married to a beautiful, young, Asian woman. I was preaching in a church that was an all black congregation. While we were waiting for my time to minister the Word, my wife suddenly instructed a young black girl to turn around and quit doing what she was doing. What that young black girl was doing was turning around to my youth pastor's wife and using her fingers to form her eyes in a slanted position. What made the situation even sadder was that the young girl was surrounded by adults who chose to ignore her actions.

These illustrations bring me to a very important point of observation. I believe that as the church goes, so goes the world. That what the church tolerates, it perpetuates. God said in Ezekiel 22:20, "I looked for a man among them to stand in the gap ... that I might not destroy the land."[16] If there is ever an area where the church has been remiss to take a stand, it is in the area of racism.

WHAT THE CHURCH TOLERATES, IT PERPETUATES.

FULFILLING THE CALL

While I do believe the church of Jesus Christ has been negligent in the area of dealing with racism, I also believe that many times it is not out of willful negligence, but rather from not knowing and understanding how to answer the call. How do we answer the call? What are some practical and biblical steps that the church and Christians can take to respond to the call to deal with racism? The answer is found in the church being willing to make certain commitments. While I don't claim to have every answer to the issue of racism, I am convinced that God has the answer to every problem and every sin that plagues humanity.

In Matthew 24, Jesus speaks to his disciples concerning various signs that speak to the spiritual and natural atmosphere that will be prevalent in the world in the last days. In verse 5, He speaks of many coming who proclaim, "I am Christ; and many will be deceived."[17] He foretells of there being wars and rumors of wars, nation rising against nation, kingdom against kingdom, and earthquakes, and famines, and pestilences. He tells His disciples that many false prophets will rise, and they will deceive many. Then He warns them (vs. 12-13), "And because iniquity shall abound, the love of many will wax cold. But he that shall endure unto the end, the same shall be saved."[18]

The next verse (v. 14), may be the most important information that Jesus gave us in this passage. He said that even with all these devastating things happening in the earth, "This gospel of the kingdom shall be preached in all the world for a witness to all nations and then shall the end come."[19] There is a lot of focus being placed on the prophetic information of the times in which we live. There is nothing wrong with that, but we must also recognize that these prophetic times are also the times of great opportunities for the gospel of the kingdom to be preached in the entire world. This is why it is so important for the church of Jesus Christ to be engaged in breaking racial barriers. I will go so far as to say that maybe the church is the reason Christ has not yet returned.

In Acts 1, after Jesus' resurrection, He told these same disciples not to leave Jerusalem, but to wait for the promise of the Father, which He had told them earlier. He said to them (Acts 1:5), "For John truly baptized with water; but ye shall be baptized with the Holy Ghost not many days hence."[20] And in Acts 2, we find the fulfillment of Jesus' promise of the Holy Spirit. We see whom He "fell on" in verses 9-11:

> "Parthians, and Medes, and Elamites and the dwellers in Mesopotamia, and in Judea, and Cappadicia, in Pontus, and Asia. Phyrgia, and Pamphylia, in Egypt, and in the parts of Lybia about Cyrene, and strangers of Rome, Jews and Proselytes, Cretes and Arabians, we do hear them speak in our tongues the wonderful works of God."[21]

These verses tell us that there were people of diverse languages and diverse dialects, and also of diverse ethnicities. As Johnny Lee Clary, a former Imperial Wizard of the Ku Klux Klan, states in his newsletter on racial reconciliation:

> "Every race that has ever existed on the face of the earth can be directly traced to these that are described in these verses. What does this mean? It is very simple. The promise of the Holy Spirit of God was not fulfilled until God gathered all races in one place to receive it."[21]

This is vital to our understanding if we are going to commit to what it takes to break down racial barriers that keep the church of Jesus Christ divided, dysfunctional and delayed from our destiny. Not only was the church established in the earth, but what happened that day changed the whole destiny of the church, and also painted a picture of what the church is supposed to be and

THE CALL | 117

how she should look. That day, when the Holy Spirit fell on the believers, the believers began to behave as believers ought to behave. They loved each other regardless of ethnicity, economic and societal position. The color of a person's skin was no longer an issue, and there were no denominational barriers as there are in today's church.

In Acts, there were those who accused the "church" of being a bunch of alcoholics. While some on the outside were amazed at what they saw and doubted, others were trying to understand what all the happenings meant (v. 12). "Others mocking said, these men are full of new wine" (v. 13). When Peter heard what they were saying, he stood up and gave the explanation (Acts 2:14-21):

"But Peter, standing up with the eleven, lifted up his voice, and said unto them, ye men of Judea, and all ye that dwell at Jerusalem, be this known unto you, and hearken to my words: for these are not drunken, as ye suppose, seeing it is but the third hour of the day. But this is that which was spoken by the prophet Joel; and it shall come to pass in the last days saith God, I will pour out of my Spirit upon all flesh: and your sons and your daughters shall prophesy, and your young men shall see visions, and your old men shall dream dreams: and on my servants and on my handmaidens I will pour out in those days of my Spirit; and they shall prophecy: and I will show wonders in the heaven above, and signs in the earth beneath; blood, and fire, and vapor of smoke: the sun shall be turned into darkness, and the moon into blood, before that great and notable day of the Lord come: and it shall come

to pass, that whosoever shall call upon the name of the Lord
shall be saved."²³

Peter is telling a group of people who didn't understand what
was going on that what they were witnessing is the result of a
promise God made before Christ laid down His life for mankind. He
ends his explanation with the most important information, "And it
shall come to pass that whosoever shall call upon the name of the
Lord shall be saved."²⁴ He informed them that salvation knows no
color lines. Salvation knows no ethnic barriers. What God did to
the church and in the church that day was so powerful that verses
42-47 record the following:

> *"And they continued to steadfastly in the apostles' doctrine*
> *and fellowship, and in breaking of bread, and prayers. And*
> *fear came upon every soul: and many wonders and signs were*
> *done by the apostles. And all that believed were together,*
> *and had all things in common; and sold their possessions and*
> *goods, and parted them to all men, as every man had need.*
> *And they continuing daily with one accord in the temple, and*
> *breaking bread from house to house, did eat their meat with*
> *gladness and singleness of heart, praising God, and having*
> *favor with all people. And the Lord added to the church daily*
> *such as should be saved."²⁵*

These verses tell us that the ultimate result of the day of
Pentecost was the kingdom of God in operation as the kingdom
of God should operate. Not some, but all who believed continued
steadfastly in the apostle's doctrine and fellowship. All who
believed were together, continuing daily with one accord in the

temple, breaking bread from house to house. All who believed did eat their meat with gladness and singleness of heart. That means that the red, yellow, black, white ... every creed and every color lived together, ate together, prayed together, and attended church together. I love this reality—they didn't do these things "once or twice a year." The Bible says they did them "daily!"

Here is the most powerful part. Verse 47 says, "Praising God, and having favor with all the people."[26] I want you to notice that because the church was behaving as the church should behave, they had favor with all the people. Because the church was loving each other the way the church should love each other, because the church refused to let anything divide it, the church of Jesus Christ had favor with "all" people. The people, who were not yet saved, liked what they saw, even if they didn't understand all they saw. Because they liked what they saw, they desired to become a part of what they saw, "and the Lord added to the church daily as should be saved."[27]

I am convinced within my soul that when the church of Jesus Christ gets her act together and breaks down every dividing wall, including the wall of racism, we will once again have favor with all the people. People will look at us, like what they see, and desire to become a part of God's wonderful kingdom. The Lord will once again add to His church daily as should be saved. But, if we are going to see this come to pass, we must be committed to doing the things God's way. Clary says this about Acts 2:47:

"The last part of verse 47 sums it all up for the true miracle of God's purpose: 'And the Lord added to their number daily those who were being saved!' Today, many churches

are crying out to God for a revival, and asking God to fill their churches, but many have not seen this happen. Could it be that the reason God has not fulfilled their request is because He is not about to place newborn Christians into a temple that allows racial, class, social, denominational, and educational divisions and barriers? Think about it!"[28]

I now ask the question, "Could it be that the reason the church as a whole struggles to have favor and there is so little church growth, is because we have forsaken what brought the church favor after the day of Pentecost?" It is time for the church of Jesus Christ to repent of racism that has kept us from winning the lost to Christ. It's time to make commitments that will allow us to do so.

ENDNOTES

1. *NIV Study Bible (Red Letter Edition).* Edited by Kenneth Barker. Grand Rapids, Michigan: The Zondervan Corporation, 1985. Print.

2. *The Hebrew-Greek Key Study Bible (King James Version).* Edited By Spiros Zodhiates, Th.D. Chattanooga, Tennessee: AMG Publishers, 1984, 1991. Print.

3. *Microsoft Encarta College Dictionary.* New York, New York: Bloombury Publishing Plc, 2001.

4. *The Hebrew-Greek Key Study Bible (King James Version).* Edited By Spiros Zodhiates, Th.D. Chattanooga, Tennessee: AMG Publishers, 1984, 1991. Print.

5. *The American Heritage Dictionary. Second Edition.* Boston, Massachusetts: Houghton Mifflin Company, 1982, 1985. Print.

6. *NIV Study Bible (Red Letter Edition).* Edited by Kenneth Barker. Grand Rapids, Michigan: The Zondervan Corporation, 1985. Print.

7. *The Hebrew-Greek Key Study Bible (King James Version).* Edited By Spiros Zodhiates, Th.D. Chattanooga, Tennessee: AMG Publishers, 1984, 1991. Print.

8. Ibid.

9. Ibid.

10. Ibid.

11. *The Message (Numbered Edition).* Ed. Eugene H. Peterson. Colorado Springs, Colorado: Navpress, 2005. Print.

12. *The Hebrew-Greek Key Study Bible (King James Version).* Edited By Spiros Zodhiates, Th.D. Chattanooga, Tennessee: AMG Publishers, 1984, 1991. Print.

13. Ibid.

14. Ocean, Billy. "The Color of Love." 1984. Web. 13 June 2013.

15. Isensee, Laura. "Criticism Follows Florida's Race-based Student Achievement Goals." The Miami Herald: Education. 13, October 2012. Web. 18 October 2012

16. *The Hebrew-Greek Key Study Bible (King James Version).* Edited By Spiros Zodhiates, Th.D. Chattanooga, Tennessee: AMG Publishers, 1984, 1991. Print.

17. Ibid.

18. Ibid.

19. Ibid.

20. Ibid.

21. Ibid.

22. Clary, Johnny Lee. *Racial Reconciliation. Preach the Cross.* 2013. Web. 28 March 2013

23. *The Hebrew-Greek Key Study Bible (King James Version).* Edited By Spiros Zodhiates, Th.D. Chattanooga, Tennessee: AMG Publishers, 1984, 1991. Print.

24. Ibid.

25. Ibid.

26. Ibid.

27. Clary, Johnny Lee. *Racial Reconciliation. Preach the Cross.* 2013. Web. 28 March 2013.

WHEN THE CHURCH OF JESUS CHRIST
BREAKS DOWN EVERY DIVIDING WALL,
INCLUDING THE WALL OF RACISM,
WE WILL ONCE AGAIN HAVE FAVOR
WITH ALL THE PEOPLE. THE LORD WILL
ONCE AGAIN ADD TO HIS CHURCH
DAILY AS SHOULD BE SAVED.

CHAPTER SEVEN

WHAT THE CHURCH MUST BE COMMITTED TO

COMMITMENT TO BIBLICAL TRUTH

"In Christ's family there can be no divisions into Jew and non-Jew, slave or free, male or female. Among us you are all equal. That is, we are in a common relationship with Jesus Christ. Also, since you are in Christ's family, then you are Abraham's famous 'descendent,' heirs according to the covenant promises."
—Galatians 3:28[1]

Those who teach and preach in our churches must be sure not to sugar-coat this passage of scripture. The words "neither Jew nor Gentile" do not just refer to the spirit man, but also to the physical man. Jesus does not want there to be spiritual lines of separation in His church, which keep women from functioning as an integral part of our ministries, nor physical lines which divide us because of the color of our skin or ethnicity. It is the color of the heart that really matters.

Growing up in a Christian home with my father serving as a pastor has afforded me the opportunity to see some wonderful works of God first hand. But, sadly, it has also allowed me to see how ugly God's children can sometimes behave. I have seen folks of all races and ethnicities walking about the kingdom of God. They represent the wonder of God's creativity, but I have witnessed too many people who claim to love the Lord—no matter the color of their skin—whose heart is black. Blackened by bitterness! Blackened by anger! Blackened by resentments! Blackened by hatred, and blackened by the spirit of racism!

Christ erased every dividing line. Paul declares in Galatians that the line has been erased—there is neither male nor female, Jew nor Greek. He did more than 2000 years ago what women's lib could not do. He made us one. A biblical church does not have one set of rules for women and another set for men. There are churches where the only time a woman is allowed in the pulpit is to bring a glass of water to the pastor. I understand that these statements do not sit well with the "supercaliLEGALISTICexpialidocious" group in the Body of Christ, but you cannot be a biblical church if you put women in bondage. That church is legalistic and bound by a spirit of religion. This same spirit used to push legalism also allows racism to dictate how we govern our churches. We need to make a commitment to biblical truth. Not only of preaching truth, but also calling those we pastor to commit to living it in every area, and that includes how we operate in the area of race relations.

In John 4 Jesus not only told his disciples to cross the ethnic and racial barriers, He told the woman at the well that the day is already here when flesh won't be an issue because now people don't worship with their flesh, but rather in spirit and in truth. He was telling her that where worship becomes real and biblical, and people are led by the spirit and not their emotions, then nothing will matter but seeing Jesus. Our languages may be different. Our body builds may be different. Our hair textures may be different, but where a church is committed to biblical truth, true worship will take place. Everything about us that is physically different will mean absolutely nothing.

COMMITMENT TO BIBLICAL RELATIONSHIP

"For the kingdom of God is not a matter of eating and drinking, but of righteousness, peace, and joy in the Holy Spirit, because anyone who serves Christ in this way is pleasing to God and approved by men."
—Romans 4:17 [2]

The kingdom of God is not about partying and having a good time. It is not about all the outward activity. It is not even about the things that make us look "churchy." The essence of what the kingdom of God is all about is right relationships. Those right relationships produce peace and joy in the Holy Spirit. The Body of Christ needs to understand and embrace the truth of the power of right relationships!

While most Bible-believing Christians would never say it, or even admit it, in our subconscious minds we believe He is a different God for each ethnic group (while holding fast to our belief that one God created all of mankind). There is a different "version" of God for the white man, and a different "version" of God for the black man … for the Asian man … the Native American man … the

Brazilian man … and so on. I know this is hard for some to believe, but if it were not true there would not be an attitude among so many Christians and those in leadership that there needs to be different churches for every ethnic group.

In many churches you can discern the dominant ethnic group by the Jesus picture they have hanging on the wall in the foyer. In some churches there is the picture of the white Jesus with blond hair and blue eyes. He's a handsome fellow. In other churches the picture shows a black Jesus with curly hair and brown piercing eyes … and He is wearing a dashiki. He is also a handsome fellow. In the church I pastor we do not hang pictures of Jesus because I do not want to send the wrong message.—if there's a picture of a black Jesus hanging on the wall, then this must be a black church and vice versa if the picture is a white Jesus. I John 3:1-2 gives us a clue concerning the futility of trying to "label" our Jesus:

> *"How great is the love the Father has lavished on us, that we should be called children of God! And that is what we are! The reason the world does not know us, is that it did not know Him. Dear friends, now we are the children of God, and what we will be has not yet been made known. We know that when He appears, we shall be like Him, for we shall see Him just as He is."* [3]

How futile and hindering it is to try and capture in our finite minds what Jesus really looks like. It's like the woman who listened to me on our radio ministry for years. One day she decided she must go to the church of the man she had been listening to faithfully for so long. She was shocked when she finally met me in person. She walked up to me and introduced herself saying, "I thought a man with such a strong and powerful voice would be much taller and heavier." I am sorry that my 5'9" and 175 pound body seemed to disappoint her. Praise to God, she was not disappointed in the sermon. Very often people hear my voice and try to imagine what I must look like. It's no different when it comes to Jesus. But, I am sure there are many who are going to be shocked when they see Jesus face to face.

This attitude many times determines who we will receive from. In our church we have a young Caucasian man who serves as our youth pastor, and a Puerto Rican man who serves as my assistant pastor. It is interesting to me that there are black and Hispanic parents who will not send their children to see our youth pastor when there is a counseling need even though they sit under his ministry weekly. The reason they give is that a white youth pastor cannot possibly understand the issues that minority youth have to deal with. Now, that is shocking to me in that when I was a youth pastor, most of the youth I pastored were Caucasian and their parents trusted me with their spiritual lives totally. You see, God is not a black God, He is not a white God, or any other color God. He is Jehovah God. Therefore, He can meet people's needs through those He has called regardless of racial and ethnic diversity. As Christians we need to make a commitment to biblical relationships that are so deep they cross the chasm of racial diversity. People come to our churches with aching hearts looking for a healing touch. We need to be one with each other to the point where they don't

GOD CAN MEET PEOPLE'S NEEDS THROUGH THOSE HE HAS CALLED REGARDLESS OF RACIAL AND ETHNIC DIVERSITY.

see us and our agendas, but rather they see Jesus deeply living inside of us.

What the church must come to understand is that everything that happens in the spirit realm requires a step be made first in the physical realm. God doesn't move in the spirit realm on our behalf until there is a predetermined movement in the physical realm on our part. Faith is not a noun, faith is a verb, and it requires action. That's why Romans 1:17 says, "The just shall live by faith."[4] God never does anything for us until we make a move in the physical. He tells us in Malachi 3:10 that if we will bring the tithe to the storehouse, He will pour out blessing that we won't have room to receive.[5] James 5:13-15 declares that if there is someone sick among us, we should call for the elders of the church.[6] The elders should anoint the sick person with oil and when the elder's pray the prayer or faith, it will heal the person who is sick. Now, what does that have to do with commitment to biblical relationship? It is that God will heal the racial breech when His children make the decision to change their thoughts and their ways in the area of race relations. When the church makes a decision mentally and physically, God will make a move spiritually. Churches have had prayer meetings for the racial tension in this nation. I am all for praying, but the time always comes when we must add action to our prayers, and in many cases prayer has been an excuse to avoid doing what God has called us to do.

I asked my church one Sunday how many of them had been out to dinner with someone outside of their ethnic group and had a meaningful conversation. Most of them had not. That was unbelievable to me. In our congregation there are more than 50 nations represented. Maslow's "The Law of the Hammer" seems to apply here: "If you have a hammer, you see every problem as nails."[7] When it comes to finding solutions to problems, the solution is usually born out of where our strength exists.

I have found in this country—especially in New England where knowledge seems to be a god—education has been both a curse and a blessing when it comes to many issues in life, specifically when it comes to dealing with racism. While education is important, and we need to be educated when it comes to dealing with racism, I fear that we have come to believe that this is the answer. We have come to believe that if we simply understand what we've been through as a nation, that knowledge alone will overcome the issue itself. Education is important, because most of the young people born in the 80s and thereafter have no clue what horrific place racism has played in shaping this nation.

When my daughters were attending high school in a suburb of Boston, most of the students who attended the school had no clue who Dr. King was and why he wrote the letter from the jail in Birmingham, regardless of their race. Even their black classmates had no clue. Education is an important tool in understanding how we became the way we are. But, bussing black kids from the inner cities to attend suburban schools and receive education was not enough to make the change that really needed to take place. The world and the church need to understand that racism is not a head problem, it is a heart problem. You cannot educate out of men's heads what is demonically driven into men's hearts. The Body of Christ gets defensive when checked in this area.

RACISM IS NOT A HEAD PROBLEM, IT IS A HEART PROBLEM.

I tell my staff consistently that we all need to be checked from time to time. We all need pats on the back, but we don't grow and recognize areas of weakness and where we need change if we're always patted on the back and never confronted with issues that hinder our growth. We grow from the ability to receive constructive criticism. The Body of Christ has been its own victim of stunted growth because we have only wanted to hear what makes us feel good. Jesus said in John 8:32, "And ye shall know the truth, and the truth will make you free."[8] Truth in this passage is the Greek word *"aletheia"* meaning, "truth that is unveiled reality; manifested."[9] When we hear the undiluted truth that is not watered down … that truth will set us free. It will liberate us. Racism is a strong demon spirit in many places in the kingdom of God. We have to face the reality that as a whole, we are not the church Jesus has commanded us to be.

What we need to do is get to the heart of the problem. We must realize that you don't change a man by simply educating his head. You can only change a man by enlightening his heart. Part of that process is understanding that genuine reconciliation is only going to happen when the Body of Christ makes up its heart and mind to actively pursue a commitment to biblical relationships. That's the way of the cross, and the way of the cross is never easy. We would rather wear a cross than bear a cross. We would rather pin a cross on our lapel than be nailed to the cross spiritually.

Hear the words of Jesus in Matthew 16:24, "Then Jesus said to His disciples, 'If any man come after me, let him deny himself, and take up his cross, and follow me …'"[10] Jesus does not instruct us to drape a cross around our necks or pin one on our lapel. He said take up our cross and follow Him. The mistake many Christians make is thinking this means to deny yourself the physical things in life. Deny yourself the luxury of driving a nice car, deny yourself the comfort of living in a nice and comfortable home, deny yourself the joy of wearing nice clothes, deny yourself ice cream or cake after dinner. If you *truly* take up your cross and follow Jesus, you will deny yourself going to the devil's picture show. You know, the place where they show movies on the big screen, especially the one called "IMAX" where the demonic movies feel real because the seats shake with the action. That is not what Jesus was talking about.

I have seen some so-called Christians deny themselves of every joy of life that they deemed to be worldly and fleshy. They don't believe in anything, and everything is of the devil. A Christmas tree is of the devil. Giving Christmas cards is of the devil. A wreath on the door is a hiding place for demons in some people's eyes. There are people who are all into the ritual and rudiments of religion that produce legalism because they misinterpret this scripture and they deny themselves of everything, thinking they are scoring points in heaven. They are convicted of certain things and they try to put their conviction on other people by masking it as a sin. They twist scriptures like this in order to back up their position. Jesus was not talking about denying yourself of things. I believe it's actually easier to do that than to do what Jesus is actually talking about here. He's not talking about the denial of stuff. He's talking about the denial of self. He's talking about our attitude, our pride. And He's talking about something deeper, about every individual Christian taking up "your" cross.

Notice He did not instruct us to take up "His cross." He said, "Take up your cross and follow me." In other words, don't do the easy stuff, do the difficult stuff. Instead of sitting in church and being a critic, spewing out negative pollution, why don't you come up with a solution? That's the way of the cross. The way of the cross is never easy.

What we've got to do is commit to breaking down any walls that exist between us and our brothers and sisters, no matter their race or ethnicities. In Ephesians 2, the Apostle Paul hits this issue on the head. History has recorded that there has always been a wall of hostility between Jews and Gentiles. They had a history of hostility for centuries. The Jews had been taught they were not only God's chosen people, they believed they were God's <u>only</u> people. Therefore, all other people were inferior and to be despised and avoided. At that time in biblical history bigotry and prejudice were socially acceptable. It was a natural part of the religious belief of biblical Palestine. Paul addresses this issue (Ephesians 2:13-16):

> *"But now in Christ Jesus to you who once were far away have been brought near through the blood of Christ. For He Himself is our peace, who has made the two one and has destroyed the barrier, the dividing wall of hostility, by abolishing in His flesh the law with its commandments and regulations. His purpose was to create in Himself one new man out of the two, thus making peace, and in this one body to reconcile both of them to God through the cross, by which He put to death their hostility."[11]*

The dividing wall applies not only to the alienation between Jews and Gentiles, which is most certainly still an issue today, but to the divisions that exist between other ethnic groups on the earth. The church must recognize that the walls are high, both inside and outside the Body of Christ. In fact, it is my experience that many times it seems higher within the church than in the world because it is masked in religious garb. But through Jesus, God broke down the wall of hostility. Therefore, He took away the church's excuse for there not being real biblical and loving relationships in this kingdom between all people who come to Him. The commitment must be biblical because that is the only way it will be genuine.

GOD BROKE DOWN THE WALL OF HOSTILITY.

In Ephesians 4:7, Paul writes, "But to each one of us grace has been given as Christ apportioned it. This is why it says: 'When He ascended on high, He led captives in His train and gave gifts to men …'"[12] He tells us that some of those gifts are apostles, some are prophets, some are evangelists, and some are pastors and teachers (v. 11). Then he tells us that the purpose of the gifts, which I believe speaks specifically to the pastors and teachers, is to prepare God's people for the works of service so that the Body of Christ may be built up.[13] The purpose of that building up is stated (v. 13), "Until we all reach unity in the faith and in the knowledge of the son of God and become mature, attaining to the whole measure of the fullness of Christ."[14]

The purpose of such gifted people Christ gives to the church is to mature the church into the fullness of Christ. The fullness is come when the church becomes in the world even as Christ would be if He were physically in the world. Then he continues to talk about the fruit of that maturity (v. 14). He says that when the church reaches this fullness in Christ Jesus, we will no longer be infants, and readily deceived by every kind of teaching that comes through the Body of Christ by men whose only goal is to deceive by scheming. He goes on to give one of the greatest proofs of spiritual maturity when he says (v. 15), "Instead, speaking the truth in love, we will all grow up into Him who is the head, that is Christ."[15] This tells us that we are to love the truth, and the proof that we love the truth that is spoken is when we don't just receive the knowledge of that truth, but begin to seek to live out that truth.

One of the great truths of God's word is found in John 13:34 where Jesus said, "A new commandment I give you; love one another. As I have loved you so you must love one another. By this all men will know that you are my disciples."[16] Jesus gave the blueprint for how Christians are to treat one another. If we are going to truly love the truth, we must embrace the truth of John 13:34 when it comes to being committed to biblical relationship. There is much at stake when it comes to our testimony to the world.

Let me explain it with my observation from growing up in a multiracial environment in high school. Whenever two black students had an argument, or even a fight, it happened because it happened. When two white students had an argument, or a fight, it happened because it happened. Likewise, when two Hispanic students had a fight or an argument, it happened because it happened. But in almost every situation where there was an argument or fight between two people of a different racial background, the first thing that came out was that the argument or fight was racially motivated.

I have observed that when disagreements, or issues occur in the Body of Christ between various races, and specifically blacks and whites, the first thing the devil initiates in most cases is the drawing of the race card. The black man declares that he is being mistreated, abused or accused because of the color of his skin. The Mexican declares his attack by the black man is because he is Mexican.

When issues arise within the church we must have biblical commitment to relationships. When that commitment is there, when problems arise, color is not brought into the equation and we deal with the real issues at hand—and we deal with those issues in a biblical way. God says to us in Isaiah 1:18, "Come now, let us reason together says the Lord."[17] If we are truly going to make a commitment to biblical relationships, we must live by the same standard as God.

A COMMITMENT TO BIBLICAL LOVE THAT EXCEEDS TOLERANCE AND ACCEPTANCE

Romans 12:9-13 reads:

> *"Love from the center of who you are; don't fake it. Run for dear life from evil; hold on for dear life to good. Be good friends who love deeply; practice playing second fiddle. Don't burn out; keep yourselves fueled and aflame. Be alert servants of the master, cheerfully expectant. Don't quit in hard times; pray all the harder. Help needy Christians; be inventive in hospitality."[18]*

Paul instructs Christians to go out of their way to show others God's love. He tells us to go out of our way as servants of the Lord. He starts out by giving us the key to accomplishing this. He says, "Love from the center of who you are; don't fake it." In other words, be sure your love is real, and not manufactured. He instructs us not to fake it. In fact, he tells us to be so invested in real love that we are creative in coming up with ways to show our love. Then He instructs (vs. 14-19):

> "Bless your enemies; no cursing under your breath, laugh with your happy friends when they are happy; share tears when they are down. Get along with each other; don't be stuck-up. Make friends with nobodies; don't be the great somebody. Don't hit back; discover the beauty in everyone. If you've got it in you, get along with everybody."[19]

Down through the years when we have talked about hard issues such as abortion, homosexuality, and racism, the mantra has been "tolerance and acceptance." Just be tolerant and accepting of people who are not like you. This all sounds wonderful and politically correct, but it presents a few problems.

First, most people can do those things without claiming to be a Christian. One can be tolerant and accepting of a person while despising them at the same time. In fact, my experience has been that in many cases those who make no claim to Christianity or religious affiliation are many times more tolerant and accepting than those who do.

Second, Paul continually reminds us throughout his writings that God has not called us to the easy street. God has not called us to be tolerant and accepting. God has called us to biblical Christian love. God has called us to something that goes far beyond acceptance and tolerance. He has called us to the place where love is the very core of our existence. To the place where love is the very force that drives our thoughts and our deeds. God does not want us to operate with a "fake it until we make it" mentality. God's desire is for His church to be so alive in Christ and Christ alive in us that we are consumed with the heart and mind of Christ. When that happens, we become inventive and creative in ways to show that love. What we need is a revelation of Jesus' love for us that is so deep that His

GOD'S DESIRE IS FOR HIS CHURCH TO BE SO ALIVE IN CHRIST AND CHRIST ALIVE IN US THAT WE ARE CONSUMED WITH THE HEART AND MIND OF CHRIST.

thoughts and ways become ours. We need a river of love flowing from us that enables us to bless our enemies, weep with those that weep, and rejoice with those that rejoice without being jealous when they are blessed.

Third, Paul exhorts us to come to a place where we are so humble and consumed with the love of Christ that we see everybody we come in contact with as somebody—a place where we seek to discover the beauty in everyone, regardless of the color of one's skin, the texture of one's hair, or the accent with which one speaks.

How can the Body of Christ accomplish this? First of all, Paul tells us in Romans 12:11 to, "Be alert servant of the master, cheerfully expectant."[20] This is something many Christians, if not most, never grasp. Let's look at the first part of Romans 12:9-19. Paul says we are to be servants. We are not to be "big shots" in this kingdom. We are to be "little shots" in the kingdom of God. The church of Jesus Christ in many places has the wrong concept of church and Christianity. So many have the attitude that we come to church and the church is here to serve us. When the truth is we are the church and we are to serve the Lord and one another. With that prior attitude comes an attitude that church is about coming in a building, singing songs, listening to sermons, and going back home. The truth is that "church" is meant to prepare us to be greater servants of the Lord and toward mankind. When a person has the heart of a servant, love does not become a challenge, but rather a way of life. Never am I closer to and more like Jesus than when I bow my knee to serve the Master. And I cannot serve the master except I serve Him through others.

Several years ago Tina Turner sang a song, "What's Love Got to Do with It?" This song was not originally written for her, but without that knowledge, one could speculate that the song was not only written for her, but by her as a way of expressing the pain she suffered at the hands of her ex-husband, Ike Turner. And, even though the song did not originate with Tina, you get the sense that she has come to a place where love is no longer relevant to that relationship or any that should arise in the future. The words are heavy and powerful. She sings, "What's love got to do, got to do with it? What's love, but a second hand emotion?" Next comes what is in my estimation the most gut wrenching part of the song, "Who needs a heart when a heart can be broken?"[21]

I understand the premise behind the words. We have all had times in our lives when we have committed our hearts fully to some sort of relationship, hoping for love and respect in return, only to find our hearts misused and abused. Lovers have had their hearts broken. Parents have had their hearts broken by children who rebelled against them, not seeing that their discipline was born out of love and protection. Children have been scarred by the abuse of parents who were supposed to love them without strings attached—some of them molested or physically abused under the guise of discipline. There are things that happen in life that can cause each of us to wonder, "What's love got to do with it? Who needs a heart when a heart can be broken?"

I submit that love has everything to do with everything in the kingdom of God. Without love the church of Jesus Christ can never truly be the church of Jesus Christ. Without love we become everything but that which we should become. We become barbarian. We become isolated. We become self-centered. We become judgmental. We become always the victim and never the victor. We become constantly defensive. We become prisoners of fear. Ultimately, we become purposeless. When a person or entity loses its purpose, it fails to operate in the original intent for its existence. The main purpose of the church of Jesus Christ is to evangelize the world by bringing the world the "Good News," the Gospel of Jesus Christ. In Matthew 28:18-20 we find what is commonly called, "The Great Commission," which Jesus gave to every believer:

> "Then Jesus came to them and said, 'All authority in heaven and on earth has been given to me. Therefore go and make disciples of all nations, baptizing them in the name of the Father and of the Son and of the Holy Spirit, and teaching them to obey everything I have commanded you. And surely I am with you always, to the very end of the age." [22]

Jesus' original intent for establishing His church on the earth was not that we might have church services and meet for social gatherings. But, rather that we might preach and teach the

Gospel—the "Good News." He instructed us to go and make disciples of all nations, all ethnos of people. The earth's population is approximately 7.05 billion people of which the overwhelming number has never been reached for the Gospel of Christ.[23] That number is near the 2.9 billion mark, making the percentage of unreached peoples by country 43.1% and individuals 41.2%. What this tells us is that we have not only a great task before us, but a great opportunity as well. That's the purpose of the church. And if we are to seize the opportunity to reach all nations, we must realize that love has everything to do with it. Only through a commitment to biblical love can we will find the power to fulfill our assignment of reaching all nations. If we simply operate through tolerance and acceptance, we can back out anytime things become difficult, there is no commitment.

John 3:16 says, "For God so loved the world that He gave His only begotten Son."[24] The premise of this scripture is based upon relationship. God so wanted relationship with fallen man that He gave His only begotten Son. Love was the motivating factor for God giving His Son, and the Son giving His life. Today, that same love is the motivating factor of the Good News. We have become religion oriented rather than relationship oriented, and the danger is that we exist to "have" church rather than "be" the church. Rather than going into all the world, we construct walls that keep us out of the world and the world from coming in to us. It is this same spirit that allows walls of racism to exist.

Let me explain a little further. In many places the church has fallen into a trap called "organized religion." Whenever a church operates out of tolerance and acceptance rather than love, it will inevitably fall into the trap of "organized religion." It is this which causes us to become "religious" instead of relationship oriented. The danger of religion is that it has the ability to look spiritual. It can display a form of godliness without power to back it up. Organized religion has so infected the church that it is normal to construct walls of separation—walls that separate from one another people God has already reached, thus keeping us from working together to reach those that God desires yet to reach. We have lost our ability to affect change in the world. "What's love got to do with it?" Everything! Love has everything to do with the kingdom of God and our assignment.

I have come to realize over the years that there are four main ways that separation exists in the church. Let me explain to you these types of separation:

1. ORGANIZED RELIGION HAS SEPARATED MALE FROM FEMALE.

I want to say that women have suffered unbelievable abuse and disrespect around the world. For too long the position has been held that women mentally, spiritually and emotionally are weaker than men. I will never forget when Bishop T.D. Jakes told of his first time experiencing the image of female genital mutilations on his first trip to Kenya. There, in an area known as West Pokot, children performed a play for him that left an indelible impression upon his heart. Dressed in their parents clothing the children enacted troubling scenes. In one scene, the father and the other man, played by boys, were bartering a goat. In the next scene the boy who played the father, who was trying to make the transaction happen, was now at home with a girl who played his wife. They were arguing about something. Through his interpreter, Bishop

Jakes learned that the mother was seeking to convince the father not to take her daughter away. Eventually, the father began to beat the mother with his shoe and run her out of the house. The short of the story is that the father snatched the girl away and took her to the marketplace. There she was handed off for the price of a goat. The interpreter explained that the purchaser might be a man of 50 or 60 years old. But, here is the terrible part. Bishop Jakes learned that usually the girl's mother would then prepare her daughter for the new husband by vaginally mutilating her so that her clitoris would be cut away in what was politely called female circumcision, but looks more (in the pictures he saw) like female castration. Bishop Jakes said, "I was shocked and disgusted by how many girls were denied even the most basic rights of growing up with their organs and passion intact." He later learned from physicians he was traveling with that many girls bled to death in the bush from castrations since they are often performed with such primitive tools as goats' horns.

I am in no way seeking to make light of the physical effect and travesty of such a practice, but when I read that, I thought, in America we should be very careful of judging these too harshly. Many a man has been guilty of castrating women emotionally and mentally in this country. In the church realm, women as a whole have been spiritually castrated for years. Since the fall in the garden, men have had a tendency even in church to devalue women. Matter of fact, it may be even more so in the church. We have twisted the Word of God in order to keep women out of key positions in the Body of Christ, and why? Because of the spirit of organized religion that has caused us to twist the truth of God's word, thus, causing the separation of male and female.

2. ORGANIZED RELIGION HAS SEPARATED CHURCH FROM CHURCH.

Organized religion has said, "I can't worship with you because you are Baptist and I am Pentecostal." Organized religion has said, "We can't share in a getting together of our churches to worship together, because if I do, you might steal some people from my church." We would be wiser, healthier, and stronger as the Body of Christ if pastors would stop all this nonsense. If people can leave you, maybe they weren't with you in the first place. I John 2:19 says, "They went out from us, but they did not really belong to us. For if they had belonged to us, they would have remained with us; but their going showed that none of them belonged to us."[25]

People leave us for different reasons. Some of them are good and right reasons, some are simply because they were never a part of us in the first place. But, when your ministry is based on organized religion rather than relationship, there is always the separating of churches from one another, and that separation limits our effectiveness.

3. ORGANIZED RELIGION HAS SEPARATED MAN FROM MAN.

I once overheard a white man and a black man having a conversation in my church one day concerning affirmative action. What piqued my curiosity was when the white man remarked how he hates affirmative action and how unfair it is to white men. The black man responded that he was also not so fond of affirmative action, but that the sad fact of the matter was that even though we have come a long way in this country in the area of race, we still need affirmative action. We need it because there are still people out there in the 21st century who will judge a man by the color of his skin rather than by the content of his character. There are people who will not hire that person, no matter how qualified he may be, because of his skin color. It is sad to say, but there are churches where minorities will not be hired, even though the pastor may desire to do so, for fear that racism may divide the body. When the church is based upon organized religion, rather than biblical relationship, man will be divided against man, which ultimately leads to the bottom line result of organized religion.

4. ORGANIZED RELIGION HAS SEPARATED BROTHER FROM BROTHER.

When I talk about brother from brother, I am talking about the saved from the unsaved. Let me mess with our organized theological thinking for a moment. What the church of Jesus Christ has done is created an "us and them" … "us against the world" atmosphere and attitude. In Matthew 6:22-23, Jesus said, "The eye is the lamp of the body. If your eyes are good, your whole body will be full of light. But if your eyes are bad, your whole body will be full of darkness. If then the light within you is darkness, how great is the darkness."[26] What Jesus is speaking to in this passage was a person's "world view." What is your world view like? In other words, the way you view the world will determine if your life is full of light or full of darkness. Your world view will determine how you view people as well. And when it comes to non-Christians, the church's world view is skewed.

We look at the unsaved as "those people out there ..." or, "those dirty rotten filthy sinners." Few people actually say it, but most Christians have this view of the unsaved even if we don't say it. We view them that way because we have a narrow world view. We see the world in light of our own place in the kingdom of God. We don't see them as we once were, as God's children who were alienated from their father because of sin and rebellion. They are our lost brothers and sisters. I know this goes against most Christians' belief systems, but please stay with me for a moment.

In John 10:11, Jesus said, "I am the Good Shepherd: The Good Shepherd lays down His life for the sheep."[27] Then in John 3:16, Jesus declared, "For God so loved the world that He gave His one and only begotten son, that whoever believes in Him shall not perish but have eternal life."[28] Let's put it together: "I am the Good Shepherd. The Good Shepherd giveth His life for the sheep." Now, we understand that He is the Good Shepherd, and the Good Shepherd gave His life for the sheep.

Who are the sheep the Good Shepherd gave his life for? The sheep are you and me, the ones who are now saved. Now, the question that we many times do not entertain is, "When did we become sheep? After we got saved or before we got saved?" If you really entertain the question, we must respond that we were sheep before we got saved. Otherwise, there would have been no need for a shepherd. There would have been no need for the Great Shepherd to lay down His life for the sheep. We need to see the correlation. Before we got saved we were sheep. We were very simply, "lost sheep!"

Matthew 9:36 says of Jesus, "When He saw the crowds, He had compassion on them, because they were harassed and helpless, like sheep without a shepherd."[29] They, like we who are saved, are sheep without a shepherd. Because of organized religion, we have become such a monster, that we don't look at people as Jesus does. We don't look at them as sheep that are lost and scattered and harassed without a shepherd. We see them as "those people" out there with spiritual leprosy. This drives home once again the message that love has everything to do with this calling to reach all nations. We have got to move from religion to relationship that is built upon biblical love.

I love the story of the little girl who was spooked one night. She came out of her room and climbed into bed between her two parents. Her daddy picked her up and took her back to her room. She said, "Daddy, I'm afraid to be alone."

He said, "Honey, don't be afraid. Jesus is with you here!"

She responded, "Daddy, that may be true, but right now I need some Jesus in the flesh."

That's what it will take if we are to deal with the spirit of racism. We need to understand that we need to become "Jesus in the flesh." In order to do that we must learn to love as Jesus did, with no strings attached.

In John 17:20-21, Jesus said, "My prayer is not for them alone. I pray for those who will believe in Me through their message, that all of them may be one, Father, just as You are in Me and I am in You."[30] It is interesting to note that even as He was about to go to the place where He would lay down His life for all and the church would be officially established on earth after His resurrection, the one thing Jesus prayed for was that His disciples would be in unity. He prayed that they would be one even as He and the Father are one. He didn't pray for them to be able to perform miracles and signs and wonders. But rather, He prayed for their unity. But then, He also prayed for those who would be watching their every move. He prayed, "For those who will believe because of their message." That prayer was not just for those disciples in that moment in time, but every subsequent disciple. That means me! That means everyone who names the name of Jesus!

Max Lucado speaks powerfully to this point:

> "Of all the lessons we can draw from this verse, don't miss the most important: unity matters to God. The Father doesn't want His kids to squabble. Disunity disturbs Him. Why? Because "All people will know that you are my followers if you love each other" (John 13:35). Unity creates belief. How will the world believe that Jesus was sent by God? Not if we agree with each other. Not if we solve every controversy. Not if we are unanimous on each vote. Not if we never make a doctrinal error. But if we love one another.
>
> Unity creates belief. Disunity fosters disbelief. Who wants to board a ship of bickering sailors? Life on the ocean may be rough, but at least the waves don't call us names."[31]

I am convinced that disunity has been Satan's master strategy to keep souls from coming into the kingdom. In fact, I believe it has been his most successful weapon. But the problem is that most people fail to see racism as a part of the enemy's strategy to keep the church in disunity. There are many things that the church has placed a higher value on than the unity of the Body of Christ. Because of this we have missed our most powerful tool of evangelism and it is unity. I believe that one of the greatest, if not the greatest sign of spiritual maturity is when a person comes to the place in Christ where they can love all people. It means loving people who may have lied about you. It means loving people who may have deserted you. It means loving people who may have turned on you. And it means loving people who are *different* than you. That is the greatest sign of spiritual maturity.

In many church circles we view the spiritually mature by the way they operate in spiritual gifts. We have this tendency to be impressed with those who have spiritual gifting. The devil has the ability to anoint people with counterfeit gifts. That is why Paul tells us in 2 Corinthians 2:11, "Lest Satan should get an advantage of us: for we are not ignorant of his devices." What we need to see is how God measures spiritual maturity. Jesus said in Matthew 7:18-20, "A good tree cannot bring forth evil, neither can a corrupt tree bring forth good fruit. Every tree that bringeth not forth good fruit is hewn down and cast into the fire. Wherefore, by their fruit ye shall know them."[32]

What is the fruit Jesus is speaking of? It is found in Galatians 5:22 where Paul says, "But the fruit of the spirit is love, joy, peace, patience, longsuffering, gentleness, goodness, faith, meekness, temperance ..."[33] Note that Paul lists all these fruits of the spirit which are signs of spiritual maturity, and it is no coincidence that love is the very first fruit mentioned. Love is not only the center of salvation, it is so powerful that without love it is impossible to walk in the other fruit of the spirit that follow.

We must understand that the Greek language has three specific words for our one word "love." There is *philia* love. That is friendship love.[34] The best way to describe this love is, by the way

WITHOUT LOVE IT IS IMPOSSIBLE TO WALK IN THE OTHER FRUITS OF THE SPIRIT.

it sounds, "fishy" or "flaky" kind of love. It's the kind of love that is based on friendship. It is a love that says, "I love you because we have something in common." This is not a terrible love, but it is basically a surface love based on conditions. It is the kind of love young people often speak of when they are dating. It's the kind of love that is based on emotion and feelings. It's the kind of love that is referred to as "puppy love." It only has true meaning in the context of how someone makes you feel. If they make you feel good, you love them. Even worse it says, "As long as you look good to me, I love you."

I heard Rich Wilkerson speak at a youth convention about the kind of love that Dave and Brenda Roever witnessed when Dave was wounded in Vietnam. Prior to that David witnessed *philia* love at its worst. While Brenda nursed David back to health, a young bride walked past his bed and then stepped to the bed of her badly burned husband and took off her wedding rings. Allegedly she placed them on his chest and said, "I have too much living to do than to remain married to someone who looks like you." Thank

God Brenda Roever understood that real love runs deeper and nursed and loved David back to health.

Then there is the *eros* kind of love.[35] This love is indicative of the love the world has today. It's probably the love that most people live by, both in the world and in the church. This is the love that says, "As long as things are going my way, I love you. As long as you don't upset me, fail me, disappoint me, or hurt me in any way I will love you. But the moment something negative occurs, my love is null and void." It's the kind of love that is derived from one finding joy in something. It also refers to what the world refers to as the first stage of falling in love. The danger here is that it can be a love that's used to control others.

But the word Paul uses for love in Galatians 5:22 is the Greek word *agape*. *Agape* is the only true translation that Christianity is built upon. It means a benevolent love. Here is a definition:

> "Love, a word not found in class. (Gr.) But only in revealed religion. Translated charity meaning benevolent love. Its benevolence, however, is not shown by doing what the person loved desires but what the one who loves deems as needed by the one loved; (e.g. For God so loved the world that He gave ... John 3:16). He gave not what man wanted, but what man needed as God perceived his need, namely His son who brought forgiveness to man. God's love for man is His doing what He thinks is best for man and not what man desires. It is God's willful direction toward man. But for man to show love to God, he must appropriate God's agape, for only God has unselfish love."[36]

Agape is a love with no strings attached. It's a love that loves in spite of. It is a love that is not earned, nor deserved. It is that love that sent our Lord and Savior to Calvary. Paul says that the fruit of the spirit begins with *agape* love. It is this love that will move God's people from the place of simply accepting and tolerating people. No marriage lasts long where people simply tolerate each other. Where couples tolerate each other, the marriage falls apart eventually because without *agape* love there is no glue.

COMMITMENT TO A BIBLICAL, PURPOSEFUL PLAN TO BREAK ETHNIC BARRIERS

Even as there must be a vision for everything a ministry wants to accomplish, churches need to have a vision that has a purposeful plan to break through ethnic barriers. Habakkuk 2:1-2 says, "I will stand at my watch and station myself on the ramparts; I will look to see what He will say to me, and what answer I am to give to this complaint. Then the Lord replied: Write the revelation (vision) and make it plain on tablets that He who readeth it may run with it."[37]

Preachers and Christians alike enjoy using this scripture when it comes to ministry and personal vision and blessing. I have no problem with that, but what would happen if every pastor took this scripture to state their position when it comes to dealing with the issue of racism? What would happen if Pastor's stood before the Lord and said, "Father, what would you desire this church to do in helping to demolish the spirit of racism in the church and in this nation?" I pose the question because I am sure that God would not only applaud us, He would surely aid us in our quest.

A thought has often come to my mind that one day as pastors stand before God, we will hear Him say something like this, "You had a wonderful vision for a nice building, a youth and children's center, and even missions. But what was your vision concerning the great commission to reach all nations and ethnicities?" I realize that I am stepping out on a limb that is a dangerous and not so popular place to be. But, there is a saying, "If you want the fruit sometimes you have to quit hugging the trunk of the tree and go out on the limb and get the fruit." So let me go after the fruit.

Proverbs 29:18 says, "Where there is no vision (revelation), the people perish…"[38] In neighborhoods everywhere, people are perishing all around us because in many churches in the kingdom of God there is little or no vision as to how we are going to reach people beyond our own ethnic groups. We must be real and acknowledge that because it is a whole lot easier and more comfortable reaching those who are most like us, as a whole we lack a vision for reaching beyond racial barriers.

I hear so often in our prayer meetings those who ask God to make their church a place where all races feel welcome. I am not against that prayer. But, we need also to ask God to give us a vision, a plan, for reaching those we want to feel welcome. When God gives us the plan, it is our responsibility to obey Him and execute the plan. The question becomes whether or not we are willing to do what we need to do in order that we might obey God's call to reach all nations. And if we are, God will give us the vision.

I was sitting in the church where Dr. J. Don George was senior pastor in September of 2012. He told of this very thing happening in his suburban Dallas, Texas congregation. Let me share with you some of the key points of his teaching.

WHAT THE CHURCH MUST BE COMMITTED TO | 153

Dr. George told of when he first came to pastor that church as a young man. It was a small church of a few hundred people. He asked God to give him a vision for the reaching of the community for Christ. God spoke to him and he began to knock on doors, to love people, and just let them know that he and the church were there to meet their needs. As he obeyed God so many years back, the church began to grow, eventually reaching around 3,000 people. Over the next years the church stayed at that level, give or take a rise and fall of a few hundred. He began to become concerned with the lack of growth in his church. He sought the Lord and the Lord said a couple of very difficult things to him. I am glad to say that Dr. George obeyed the Lord and as a result the church has recently grown to 10,000 weekly worshippers. But, let me share the one thing God told him he must change. He shared how God told him his church was too white!

This troubled J. Don George because he was not a man who was racist. His church had done great ministry in many of the black neighborhoods around Dallas, and there were a few black people attending his church. The problem was that his church did not reflect the area that surrounded it. So he had to make the necessary adjustments so the church body was a reflection of the local community. What I want to stress is that Dr. George asked God for a vision and God gave it to him. His church and ministry were rewarded for their obedience. He came to that church as a young man in his twenties, fresh out of college. Now, as a faithful and seasoned pastor in his seventies, he and his church are experiencing their greatest season in the history of that congregation. I ask, "What might God do in our communities if every pastor would genuinely ask God for a vision that breaks racial barriers?"

COMMITMENT TO BIBLICAL COMMPASSION THAT MAKES US SENSITIVE TO ALL OF GOD'S PEOPLE

I want to share several scriptures with you concerning Jesus as a backdrop for this point:

Matthew 9:36 says this of Jesus: *"When He saw the crowd, he had compassion on them, because they were harassed and helpless, like sheep without a shepherd."*[39]

Matthew 14:14 says: *"When Jesus landed and saw the large crowd, he had compassion for them and healed their sick."*[40]

Matthew 15:32 says: *"Jesus called His disciples to Him and said, 'I have compassion for these people; they have already been with Me three days and have nothing to eat. I do not send them away hungry, or they may collapse on the way."*[41]

Matthew 20:34 says: *"Jesus had compassion on them and touched their eyes. Immediately they received their sights and followed Him."*[42]

I want to go back to Matthew 14:14 where it speaks to the reality that when Jesus saw the large crowd, He had compassion on them. The compassion He felt so moved Him that He healed them. The Bible also records that as evening was approaching, Jesus' disciples came to Him and stated that with the area being such a remote area, it would be good to send the crowds away so they could go to the villages and buy themselves some food. I want you to see this clearly. These are the same disciples who saw Jesus moved with such a heart of compassion that it caused Him to spend hours praying for them and healing them. They witnessed Him do the "impossible" before their eyes. Yet, when it came to the "possible" they wanted to send the same people away hungry.

I love Jesus' response. Jesus replied (v. 16), "They do not need to go away. You give them something to eat."[43] In other words, why don't you behave like me and become a servant. Show some compassion instead of simply talking about it. Every scripture that I shared with you speaks to the compassionate heart that Christ has. Thus, we see the dilemma of the church today when it comes to the issue of race. We must gain the heart of God, which is the compassion of Jesus in order to deal with this issue. What we need to understand is that the truest measure of love is compassion. We don't truly step over into the revelation of the cause of Calvary, to why Jesus died for us, until we are moved with hearts of compassion.

TO DEAL WITH RACISM WE MUST GAIN THE HEART OF GOD.

Colossians 3:12 says, "Therefore, as God's chosen people, holy and dearly beloved, clothe yourselves with compassion, kindness, humility, gentleness and patience."[44] I believe that God had Paul often place words in strategic order when he wrote His books. It follows that if you get compassion, it will give birth to kindness, humility, gentleness and patience. Then Ephesians 4:32 gives this admonition, "Be kind and compassionate to one another."[45] 1 Peter 3:8 tells us, "Finally, all of you, live in harmony with one another, be sympathetic, love as brothers, be compassionate and humble."[46]

Compassion means, "a deep feeling or sharing the suffering of another, together with the inclination to give aid or support or to show mercy."[47] Compassion, like love, is not a noun. Compassion is a verb. It is not a descriptive noun as in naming something, it is an action verb. It commands a demonstrative response. Action is a fruit of compassion. Another fruit of compassion is sensitivity. Notice that one of those definitions of compassion is that of a deep feeling of sharing in the suffering of another. We seem to be a world that is becoming more and more desensitized to suffering and people's pain. I am amazed and appalled at how often fights and other acts of violence are recorded on YouTube. And it seems that with all the progress that has been made in the area of race relations, for every step we take forward, we fall back two.

Let me cite some modern day happenings that testify such insensitivity. On February 11, 2009, the *Washington Post* ran an article which revealed Olympic men's basketball players from Spain who defended a photo in an ad showing players using their fingers to apparently make their eyes slant to look more Chinese.[48]

Another example of a lack of sensitivity and one of the most appalling things to me in our day and age is the use of the word "nigga" by youth. I realize that it's popular to use "nigga" when young people refer to their "boy," or their "homie." What concerns me more is that Christian young people use this word with the same freedom as the youth outside the body of Christ. I have heard not only young people in the church I pastor use it, I have heard youth pastors use it in order to seek to fit in with the youth culture of this day. Youth pastors and parents need to understand that we are Christians and need to teach our youth this reality in the way they not only conduct themselves physically, but verbally as well. Youth need to be taught that their terminology is offensive first to God, and then to many people. As a black man, I am offended when black people use the word.

I remember growing up and listening to relatives joke by using the slang, "nigga please." I walk through the malls and I hear white kids, black kids, Asian kids, Hispanic kids, and kids of all ethnicities who say to one another, "What's up my nigga!" They treat it simply as part of their everyday common greeting with one another. I have heard black people call one another by the same derogatory name. And when I confront them concerning how offensive their verbiage is, they whitewash it by saying, "Well, anybody can be a 'nigga' because it means to act like a fool, or whatever."

What they need to realize is that is not what the word really means. I know that people try to excuse it by saying that it is a derivative of the other word ending in "r." We need to understand that it is not really truly derived from the same word. Neither does it mean to act like a fool. That word, "nigger" is really a term used to define a stingy person. The word that is meant to stand for a foolish acting person is actually "to act niggardly."[49] Nevertheless, what we need to realize is that any form of usage is offensive. We would do good to remember that 1,000s of black people were hung from trees, burned alive, and some had their skulls bashed in while being called that derogatory name.

I remember the day when it was kosher for black people to refer to one another with this terminology. But, if someone white said it, they would beat them up, or worse. This word, or any other racially derogatory word used to communicate with another ethnicity is wrong, no matter what the context we use to justify it. Let's look at another explanation of this terminology:

> "This term is arguably the most offensive racial slur in the English language. The fact that African Americans and other people of color sometimes use the word in reference to themselves does not excuse its present day use by members of other ethnic groups. White students may be accustomed to hearing it in pop context. They should avoid using it, even in fictional dialogue. Those who persist in using it should remember that their use of the word reflects directly upon them, the users. The terms of choice are African American, black person, or person of color."[50]

Let me say again that all people, especially Christians should not use any racially derogatory names, even with their own ethnic group. And there is never a proper time to use the word "nigga" in any relationship as Christians. I also want to state that though I am a black man and proud to be such, my term of choice is simply "American." My ancestors did not die for me to have to live in America by a label. I am an American who is black. It even bothers me that for the sake of interpretation to have to use the terms "white" or "black" in this thesis to describe God's creation.

Jesus had something powerful to say about words in Matthew 12:34-37:

> *"You have minds like a snake pit! How do you suppose what you say is worth anything when you are so foul-minded? It's your heart, not the dictionary that gives meaning to your words. A good person produces good deeds and good words season after season. An evil person is a blight on the orchard.*

Let me tell you something: Every one of these careless words is going to come back to haunt you. There will be a time of reckoning. Words are powerful; take them seriously. Words can be your salvation. Words can be your damnation."[51]

Proverbs 18:21 says, "The tongue has the power of life and death, and those who love it will eat its fruit."[52] Let's look at the same passage from another translation, "Words kill, words give life: they're either poison or fruit, you choose."[53] It's what is in our hearts that determines what comes out of our mouths. I pray that we allow God to give us hearts of compassion that birth sensitivity in us that goes beyond the color of people's skin. If what I am writing offends you, I hope that it offends you enough to speak out against it. This kind of language and attitudes are upheld in many of our churches.

One of the surest ways to become sensitive in the area of racism is to place oneself in the shoes of another. Years ago, as a child, I would hear many people repeat an old Native American saying, "Don't criticize me until you have walked a mile in my moccasins." I did not understand it growing up, but I now know that they meant, "Be careful how you judge someone until you have had to go through what they have gone through." I also think that it was an invitation to put oneself in another man's position; to literally take on the feelings of that person, to become emotionally engaged in what that person is feeling. I believe that is what Dr. King was driving at when he penned these words while locked up in a jail cell in Birmingham, Alabama:

"Perhaps it is easy for those who have never felt the stinging of the darts of segregation to say 'wait.' But when you have seen vicious mobs lynch your mothers and fathers at will and drown your sisters and brothers at whim; when you have seen hate-filled policemen curse, kick, brutalize, and even kill your black brothers and sisters without impunity; when you see the vast majority of your 20 million negro brothers smothering in an airtight cage of poverty in the midst of an affluent society; when you suddenly find your tongue twisted and your speech stammering as you seek to explain to your six-year-old daughter why she can't go to the public amusement park that has just been advertised on television, and see tears welling up in her little eyes when she is told that Funtown is closed to colored children, and see the depressing clouds of inferiority begin in her little mental sky, and see her begin to distort her little personality by unconsciously developing a bitterness toward white people … when you take a cross-country drive and find it necessary to sleep night after night in the uncomfortable corners of your automobile because no motel will accept you; when you are humiliated day in and day out by nagging signs reading, 'white' men and 'colored'; when your first name becomes 'nigger' and your middle name becomes 'boy' (however old you are)… and when your wife and mother are never given the respected title of 'Mrs.'; when you are harried by day and haunted by night by the fact that you are a negro, living constantly at tip-tie stance never quite knowing what to expect next, and plagued with inner fears and outer resentments; when you are forever fighting a degenerating sense of 'nobodiness'; then you will understand why we find it difficult to wait."[54]

What Dr. King was seeking to drive home is the reality that even in this day in which we live, we must be careful not to make light of what black people have been through. We need to be sensitive to other people's plight. And the only way to walk in that kind of compassion and sensitivity is to somehow allow the Holy Spirit to cause us to feel what others feel.

The Holy Spirit taught me this lesson one Sunday when I was preaching a message about giving. I made the statement, "Don't be an Indian giver," during a point I was trying to make that morning. After the service, a man whom I had never seen before came up to me and told me how he enjoyed the service but that he was offended by my Indian giver remark. I responded by saying that I meant no harm and that it was a statement I grew up hearing all my life. He said he understood, but as a Native American it was offensive to him. He proceeded to explain to me that he understood what "my people" had been through, but felt that his people had suffered even more than mine. Where I come from, in Illinois, that statement is commonly used by Native Americans and all other Americans alike. I don't know that I have ever used that statement again since that day. But I do know that it taught me that whether I agreed with him or not, I needed to be sensitive to why that statement bothered him.

As time went on I became aware that a lot of his pain came from being adopted into a white family and believing all his life that he was white, all while being abused and beaten by his alcoholic, adopted father. When he found out he was Native American, the river of rage began to flow. This man was so angry with life that he came to church one day with a gun in his pocket with the intent of killing me because I missed an appointment with him at the local donut shop due to a snow storm. That Sunday morning several deacons had to physically remove him from the foyer of the church.

That day as I preached two Sunday morning services, I could see him from the platform as he continued to pace across the street for 4.5 hours waiting to "kill" me. That day my deacon board snuck my family and I out the back door of the church to assure that we got home safely.

The following Wednesday, my administrative assistant informed me that my would-be killer was on the telephone asking to speak to me. I reluctantly took his call. As we were talking he asked me a silly question. He asked, "You do know I was mad at you Sunday, don't you?" After which he followed up by asking if it would be alright if he came to church that evening. I sat there on the other end of the phone, stunned, not believing that the one who threatened to kill me only a few days ago was now asking if he could come to church. As I struggled, the Holy Spirit spoke to me to let him come. I informed him that he could attend, but we would be watching him closely and that he could only come if he stayed away from threatening people.

After I finished speaking with him I called up one of my deacons who had helped remove this man from the sanctuary that prior Sunday. That deacon's words still ring as loudly in my ear as they did nearly 17 years ago. He responded, "Pastor, I love you, but have you lost your cotton pickin' mind?" That night that man who was such an angry young man, sat in the middle of the sanctuary during service, arms folded across his chest and a scowl on his face the whole time I was preaching. At the end of the service, I heard the spirit instruct me to not close with prayer but rather to close the service by allowing people to come forward and worship the Lord until they felt the Holy Spirit release them. As the worship continued and people began to depart, I saw this young man get up from his seat and begin to move slowly toward the platform as I led the few who remained in worship. As he moved, deacons began to move. But, I felt in my spirit to instruct them to let him approach. He got to the front of the altar area and just stood there with his arms folded and that same old scowl on his face. After most of the people had left, I stepped off the platform and reached out my hand to him. He reached back, took my hand, held it tightly and said, "I have a bone to pick with you." I responded, "Oh, really?" He said, "Yes! You didn't give an altar call and I am ready to give my heart to Jesus." The short of the story is that he wept his way into the kingdom through the saving power of Jesus that night. He told me how God drew him because he watched as I loved him in spite of his anger and the remarks he had made concerning his people going through more than mine had been through.

HE WEPT HIS WAY INTO THE KINGDOM THROUGH THE SAVING POWER OF JESUS.

I share this story because it speaks to the power of what the Holy Spirit can do if we will just allow Him to give us hearts of compassion for all people. You see in my eyes, my people had suffered far greater than the Native Americans had. In his eyes it was quite the opposite. And it is interesting that to this day we both have a greater compassion for what each group has gone through. What changed me was allowing the Holy Spirit to put me in His place of feeling through compassion.

Let me share a couple experiences that show the personal pain we can cause when we are insensitive to one another. One of the reasons I am so against even my own race of people using the word "nigga" is that it gives many people the impression that all black people are comfortable with such terminology. And thus, gives those who are close friends the license to tell racial jokes. I will never forget the day when I heard a young white man take the words to an old children's church song and add an offensive twist to it and sing it to one of his black friends. He rewrote the song, "Jesus Loves the Little Children" with a racial message to it. The original wording is as follows:

"Jesus loves the little children, all the children of the world

Red and yellow, black and white, they are precious in His sight

Jesus loves the little children of the world"

Here is the version the young white man sang:

"Jesus loves the little children, all the children of the world

Niggers, chinks, and Jews and wops, Jesus thinks they're really tops

Jesus loves the little children of the world"

And they laughed about it as though it was no big deal. But, there are at least a couple issues involved here. The first issue is that while his one black friend my not have been offended, most minorities would be offended. The second issue is that Christians should avoid making careless jokes.

Early in my walk with the Lord I had been guilty myself of sharing jokes concerning different races of people that may have been hurtful even to the people who laughed with me. Many times I hear people of different ethnicities share jokes with one another, about one another, that pertain to race or skin color. While I do not agree with it, I understand that in many racial relationships this is the way that some try to make it clear that they are comfortable with one another and that they have no issue with race. It is the attitude of "taking our relationship seriously, while not taking ourselves seriously." That is all well and good, but as Christians we must weigh not just our actions, but our words in light of what our testimony is to be to the world. There is a time when we must all mature and realize that there are some things in life, no matter how innocent they seem to be, that have the potential to cause great pain.

In Colossians 4:6, Paul gives this admonishment, "Let your conversation be always full of grace, seasoned with salt, so that you may know how to answer everyone."[55] Another translation says, "Be gracious in your speech. The goal is to bring out the best in others in a conversation, not to put them down, not cut them out."[56] Then we see in Colossians 3:17 where Paul says, "And whatever you do, whether in word or deed, do it all in the name of the Lord Jesus, giving thanks to God the Father through Him."[57] Finally in Philippians 1:27, Paul says, "Meanwhile, live in such a way that you are a credit to the message of Christ."[58] It is very clear that our sensitivity must be not only in what we do, but also in what we say. Our whole life belongs to God. Therefore, we must glorify Him in words as well as actions.

Let me close this point with an illustration of how insensitive actions can cause pain. For years my wife has been alienated by her parents because of personal issues that they refuse to acknowledge and seek to resolve. After 20 years of separation and no phone calls, my father-in-law called to inform us that my wife's mother's health was not well. After much thought and prayer, we went to visit her parents. One evening after we left the nursing home where her mom was living, my father-in-law asked us to come to the house to go through some old pictures. As we looked through the pictures, I noticed a particular picture hanging on the wall. Intrigued, I moved closer to get a better look because I thought my eyes were playing tricks on me. But to my dismay, my eyesight was accurate. There on the wall was a picture of my father-in-law dressed as a woman and painted in blackface. When I asked him about it, he lightly informed us that it was a Dutch tradition at Christmas time to do a skit that entails a person portraying a black person. My mother and father-in-law I do not doubt are Christians and love God dearly, but it never once crossed their minds that not only might their black son-in-law be offended, but that their adopted daughter who went through years of pain in grade school because of the color of her skin might be offended.

May God help all His children to be sensitive to the feelings of others, both in word and deed.

COMMITMENT TO BIBLICAL ACCEPTANCE

This may sound like a contradiction to something I said earlier when I spoke about the need to go beyond tolerance and acceptance. We need to understand what is God's definition and what is the world's definition are often light years apart when we deal with many issues. When I said one problem with the church is that we are high on acceptance and tolerance and God has not called us to be tolerant and accepting, I was talking about the way most people define these issues.

Here is my definition: Biblical acceptance means that ultimately we celebrate our differences rather than tolerating them. Romans 15:7 says, "So reach out and welcome one another to God's glory. Jesus did it; now you can do it."[59] In other words, we have got to stop placating one another simply to make people feel better. Here's what I mean, we have got to stop saying, "I don't see color!" The truth of the matter is that we do see color, actually. I know what people mean when they make that statement. They are trying to express with sincerity of heart that the color of a person's skin means nothing to them, that skin color does not dictate how we feel about a person. But, here is the problem with that line of thinking. Firstly, it is impossible to *not* see color unless you are scientifically and medically color blind. Yet, somehow even the color blind can see clearly when it comes to race. Secondly, I don't want to not see a person's skin color. I don't want to *not* see that the texture of our hair is different. I don't want to *not* notice the different features that are inherent to one ethnicity or another. I am not sure if God even wants us to not see them. Why else would He have created the differences if He didn't want us to experience and enjoy them?

I want to see what makes people who have so much in common different because I want to celebrate those differences. When we celebrate one another we celebrate the creativity of our awesome God. What is different about each of us is what shows off God's great and awesome power and glory. Not only do the magnitude of variations of birds and plants, animals and trees, flowers and stars show how awesome He is, but mankind speaks more than any other thing in creation concerning the creative power of our great God. In Genesis 1:26-28 we find these words:

"Let us make human beings in our own image, make them reflecting our nature so they can be responsible for the fish in the sea, the birds in the air, the cattle, and trees, the earth itself. And every animal that moves on the face of the earth."[60]

"God created human beings; He created them godlike, reflecting God's nature. He created them male and female."[61]

When we celebrate what is different about mankind, we are acknowledging that the God who created every man and woman did so in His image and likeness. Yet, He gave us this vast array of beautiful human beings who are so godlike, but, yet so different in appearance. All the differences in the universe do not change this one fact: we are all made in God's likeness.

When I look at all the differences in skin tones and textures of hair, when I recognize the different shapes in noses and ears of which each have their own form indicative to certain nationalities, then I am humbled when I realize that 99.9% of every persons DNA is the same. Only 0.1% sets us apart: our fingerprint.[62] Therefore, I want to recognize and celebrate those things which are different about us because what is different is what makes our existence so wonderful.

If mankind every really thought about just how creative, powerful, and thoughtful God is that He could and would create so many ethnic groups, we would truly be humbled by our differences rather than arrogant and pumped with foolish pride. We know that when we get saved, the real person we are is restored once again into the very image and likeness of God. I'm so glad God gave us this wonderful gift of different physical appearances that makes what is just alike different. That's the "God kind" of acceptance that we need if the church is to attack the enemy of racism, both in the church and in the world.

COMMITMENT TO BIBLICAL SACRIFICE

Hebrews 12:2-3 records these words:

> "Let us fix our eyes on Jesus, the author and perfector of our faith, who for the joy set before Him endured the cross, scorning shame, and sat down at the right hand of throne of God. Consider Him who endured such opposition from sinful men, so that you will not grow weary and lose heart."[63]

It is well past time for the Body of Christ to be willing to pay the price of sacrifice needed to break the spirit of racism. The tendency with mankind is to believe that some things will simply always exist. Therefore, it is not worth the effort to seek to make a difference. There is the prevailing attitude that "we have come a mighty long way," and so many have already sacrificed so much, yet this issue remains. Therefore, the effort is not worth the sacrifice in the long run. I need to say this again: God did not give the call of reconciliation to the government. Neither did He give it to the White House. He gave the call to His church.

IT IS WELL PAST TIME FOR THE BODY OF CHRIST TO BE WILLING TO PAY THE PRICE OF SACRIFICE NEEDED TO BREAK THE SPIRIT OF RACISM.

If we are going to answer the call, the church must not only be willing, but must also understand that there is a sacrificial price that must be paid in order to break the demon power of racism. For pastors, it may cost them members of their church. You see, the power of the kingdom is found in unity. I mentioned this earlier where Psalm 133:1 speaks to the power of unity.[64] And Jesus said in John 13:35 that the only way men will know we are His disciples is by our love for one another.[65] He didn't mention our programs, or our wonderful buildings. He said that the giveaway to show we are His disciples is the love that we have for one another. God places the highest priority on unity. The reason is that God created the kingdom to operate through connectivity.

What God loves, Satan hates. God loves unity. Satan hates it. His hatred is so strong when it comes to unity that you can rest assured the moment pastors stand for righteousness in the area of racism, there will be some members whom the enemy will use to resist the stance. There will be those who have the attitude that says, "When those people start coming in this church, we are moving to a new church."

One day a pastor friend of mine told me of a pastor who told his board that God had given him a vision to reach their city for Christ. Part of that vision would require them to start busing inner city children into their nice suburban church. One board member piped up and let the pastor know that in no uncertain terms if he started doing that, soon those kids' parents would want to come to their church as well. "Isn't that the point?" the pastor replied. The board member became enraged and informed the pastor that the black kids need to go to their own churches. When the pastor addressed his attitude as being racist, the board member informed him, "I ain't no racist. I have several black men who work for me. I work with them five days a week and eat lunch with them. But I don't have to worship with them on Sunday. But I ain't no racist. And if you bring them here, me and my family are leaving."

You guessed correclty, they left. That family not only left, but the pastor told them they were free to leave because he believed it was better to obey God than man. He lost some other families as well. But for those he lost, God gave him twice as many in their place.

I was in a conference several years ago where I heard Dr. John Maxwell make a statement to this effect: "Everybody has the potential to bless you. Some by staying. Some by going." For some attendees it may mean losing fake friends. As hard as it may be to believe, in the 21st century we still have those who call out ungodly names to those who have the courage to cross the color lines. One of the nicer names I have been called for being willing to connect with my white pastoral brethren is "Oreo cookie." Meaning, I am black on the outside but white on the inside. And if a white pastor connects with a black pastor, there are still those, even in the Body of Christ who use that worn-out civil rights war rhetoric to inform them that they are a "certain kind of lover."

That's part of the price tag when standing up for righteousness. I ask how we dare not to accept our assignment? Would we rather choose comfort after what Jesus went through that we might be reconciled back to the Father? If we are to really be a person who brings about effectual change, we must put ourselves in the place of those who are going through the pains until we in essence feel what the person feels. In order to do that we must put ourselves in Jesus' place and feel the pain that He feels when it comes to the issue of racism. The truth is that if we neglect to put ourselves in the same position, we have not fully appreciated and embraced the sacrifice Christ made on our behalf. Jesus' whole attitude was that of sacrifice. Ours must be the same if we are to attack the demon spirit of racism. It may cost some pastors members in the short run. It may cost parishioners some friendships as well. Righteousness almost always seems to be loss initially.

In Genesis 39, we find the story of Joseph. He is serving in authority under Potiphar. And Potiphar's wife makes advances to him. His response to those advances are recorded (vs. 8-9):

> "But he refused and said to his master's wife, 'Behold, with me here, my master does not concern himself with anything in the house, and he has put all that he owns in my charge. There is no one greater in this house than I, and he has withheld nothing from me except you, because you are his wife. How then could I do this great evil, and sin against God?'"[66]

The rest of the story records that as she physically advances toward him, she grabs his coat and he wiggles out of it and flees. She in turn creates a false story accusing Joseph of trying to rape her. Joseph ends up in prison for a period of time. From the palace to the prison for seeking to do what was righteous. He suffered greatly in the short run for his sacrificial stance for righteousness. He eventually became the second most influential leader in the most powerful nation in ancient Israel. Commitment to biblical sacrifice when it comes to this issue of racism may seem to cause some loss in the short run, but we will be rewarded in the long run.

Let me give one more word to how we stand in the pulpit and proclaim the glorious Gospel of Jesus Christ. We do not have the luxury of choosing which parts we will or will not proclaim. We do not have the luxury of proclaiming only the words we are comfortable with. Dr. Dean Register says that a preacher has four orders.[67] They are found in 2 Timothy 4:1-5. They are Paul's direction to a young up and coming preacher named Timothy. Paul told Timothy:

1. A PREACHER IS ORDERED TO PROCLAIM GOD'S WORD.

The preacher is to preach God's word; not in his opinion, nor what seems popular. I Timothy 4:1-2a says, "In the presence of God and of Christ Jesus, who will judge the living and dead, and in view of His appearing and His kingdom, I give you this charge: preach the word."[68] Notice he did not say "a" word but "the" word. He instructed Timothy to not "Mickey Mouse" around the word but to preach "the" word.

2. A PREACHER IS COMMANDED TO CARRY OUT HIS ASSIGNMENT WITH DISCIPLINE.

In verse 2b, Paul says, "Be prepared in season and out ..." Paul's counsel is to be prepared. Don't take this assignment to preach the word lightly. Take time to study the word of God and be prepared spiritually as well. In other words, he wanted Timothy to understand that "inspiration comes after perspiration." If we will study and prepare "the" word, God will supply the anointing to change people's hearts.

3. A PREACHER IS CHARGED TO RESCUE THE PERISHING.

In verse 2c, Paul says to, "Correct, rebuke, and encourage-with great patience and careful instruction ..." Paul instructs Timothy to be careful not to fall in the trap of preaching what the people want to hear, but to preach what they need to hear. There will be times when our preaching cannot just be encouragement. There will be times when it must bring correction. I believe that sometimes the "Good News" is "painful news" before it becomes "good news" to some.

4. A PREACHER IS WARNED THAT MANY WILL NOT EMBRACE GOD'S TRUTH.

In Verse 3, Paul tells young Timothy, "For the time will come when men will not put up with sound doctrine. Instead, to suit their own desires, they will gather around them a great number of teachers to say what their itching ears want to hear." In verse 4, Paul says, "They will turn their ears away from the truth and turn aside to myths." But then he encourages Timothy in verse 5 by saying, "But you, keep your head in all situations, endure hardships, do the work of an evangelist, discharge all the duties of your ministry."

Paul instructed Timothy to guard against becoming discouraged and giving up in spite of the fact that many will not receive the true word and in spite of the fact that they will run after fables and myths. He told him to do what needs to be done in spite of opposition, to preach the word in spite of opposition. Teach the truth even though there will be those who reject it.

At the end of the day our desire should be to end as Paul did. In 2 Timothy 4:6, he tells Timothy that he is leaving him these instructions for his time to depart this life is at hand.[69] Then he tells Timothy the way a preacher needs to leave when his assignment is over. In verse 7 Paul says, "I have fought the good fight, I have finished the race, I have kept the faith. Now there is in store for me the crown of righteousness, which the Lord, the righteous judge, will award to me on that day—and not only me, but also to all who love His appearing."[70] That's the goal of preaching this word, to be found faithful to God and His word even when it is not a popular word.

THE GOAL OF PREACHING THE WORD IS TO BE FOUND FAITHFUL TO GOD AND HIS WORD EVEN WHEN IT IS NOT A POPULAR WORD.

What Paul conveys to Timothy, I desire to convey to all who stand in the pulpit. If we are going to break the demonic spirit that drives racism in the Body of Christ, above everything else that we are committed to, we must be committed to preaching the word. We must be strong enough to preach for the "cause rather than the applause." If we will be faithful to preach the truth of God's word, the Holy Spirit will be faithful to cause the word to penetrate the hardness of men's hearts.

Psalm 107:20 says, "He sent forth His word and healed them ..."[71] Psalm 103:3 says, "Who forgives all your sins and heals all your diseases."[72] Racism is the result of the disease called sin and only the word can heal man of this infection caused by the disease of sin.

COMMITMENT TO BIBLICAL HONESTY

Ephesians 4:15 says, "Instead, speaking the truth in love, we will in all things grow up into Him who is the head, that is Christ."[73] Then in John 8:32 it is recorded to the Jews who had believed Him, Jesus said, "Then you will know the truth, and the truth will set you free.'"[74] And in John 15:15 Jesus said, "No longer do I call you servants, for a servant does not know what his master is doing; but I have called you friends, for all things that I have heard from my Father I have made known to you."[75]

I simply find it amazing that Jesus calls us friends. You see, real friends can be trusted and that includes their words. What I am pointing to is the reality of a person saying what he means and meaning what he says. We have in the world, and in the church what I would call an abundance of "spiritual patronizing." Nowhere is this practiced more than in religious circles. Whether you are a Christian or a Muslim; a Catholic or a Methodist; a Baptist or a Presbyterian; there is one thing all religious groups have in common: we are taught to say all the right stuff. We have been taught to say and do the stuff that Christians should say and do. Hug everybody. Play the sloppy agape games of hugging and greeting one another with a holy kiss. And, of course it must be wrapped up in the theme of Christianity, "I love you."

In the world, the words "I love you" have become nothing more than empty vocabulary. Young boys with their hormones racing at 120 miles per hour tell every young girl who is silly enough to let him close enough to whisper in her ear, "I love you." The truth is they don't have one iota of an idea what love really is. They remind me of a dog running down the road, chasing a car and barking at it, as if to let the car know how badly they want it. But, once they catch it, they don't know what to do with it. Young boys haven't even learned to love themselves enough that it would cause them to take a daily shower, put on some deodorant and brush their teeth regularly … much less knowing how to truly love someone else yet. In the world, love has become just another way of saying, "I need something from you. You have what I want. Ooh baby, you got what I need. And if I tell you I love you just the right way and enough times, you'll give me what I want." Here's the problem, that's phony and insincere.

If we were to be honest, we must admit that in the Body of Christ, we too have so watered down the meaning of love. To the point that when we say the words "I love you" as we hug one another, most of the time it is void of true sincerity. If we were really walking in biblical, Holy Spirit, anointed love, some Christians would not be so mean. I'm amazed at how many Christians can so easily say, "I love you," and just as easily attack the very people we say we love.

What I see is that if we are going to break down racial walls and whatever walls we have built that the enemy seeks to use to keep the kingdom of God divided, we have got to get serious about being sincere. For where there is sincerity, there will be trust and credibility. We need to understand that there are some people who can so easily tell you with their lips to your face they love you. But, you can see that it is so true that the eyes are the window to the soul, because even as the words roll off their lips, their eyes betray the reality of their heart. Soon their actions betray their words. People need to know that when they come through the doors of our churches there is not one thing portrayed from our mouths while there is something completely different displayed behind their backs.

When I became the pastor of my present ministry, one minority who was a board member at that time, related to me his personal experience. He told of overhearing the former pastor telling another deacon how important it was that the church had enough minorities in leadership in order to draw more minorities to the church. Allegedly, the deacon responded by saying, "Good! Every board needs its token minorities." If that was indeed a true conversation, then it is a clear cut example of what happens when a church is not committed to biblical honesty. For indeed this story does not match the messages I have heard preached from the pulpit in the past. Most pastors at some time or another preach heavy messages concerning love and deep compassion. But, often we do not demand that those in our leadership seek to live the messages we preach. Though there were more minorities added to that deacon board, and I am a minority pastor, it has taken years to remove the stigma and subtle division that existed in the leadership.

COMMITMENT TO BIBLICAL INTEGRITY OF GOD'S WORD

In Romans 2:13-24, Paul writes these words:

> *"For it is not those who hear the law who are righteous in God's sight, but it is those who obey the law who will indeed be declared righteous. (Indeed, when gentiles, who do not know the law, do by nature things required by the law, they*

are a law for themselves, even though they do not have the law, since they show that the requirements of the law are written on their hearts, their consciences also bearing witness, and their thoughts now accusing, now defending them.) This will take place on the day when God will judge men's secrets through Jesus Christ, as my gospel declares. Now you, if you call yourself a Jew; if you rely on the law and brag about your relationship with God; if you know His will and approve of what is superior because you are instructed by the law; if you are convinced that you are a guide for the blind, an instructor of the foolish, a teacher of infants, because you have in the law the embodiment of knowledge and truth – you then who teach others, do you not teach yourself? You who preach against stealing, do you not steal? You who say that people should not commit adultery, do you commit adultery? You who abhor idols do you rob temples? You who brag about the law, do you dishonor God by breaking the law? As it is written: "God's name is blasphemed among the gentiles because of you."[76]

Dr. J. Vernon McGee makes this observation concerning this passage of scripture:

"I hear it said that the heathen are lost because they haven't heard of Christ and haven't accepted Him. My friend, they are lost because they are sinners. That's the condition of all mankind. Men are not saved by the light they have; they are judged by the light they have. God can and will judge the heathen by his own conscience. Some folk think because the heathen do not have the revelation of God that they will escape God's judgment. But the fact is that they are not living up to the light they have. God will judge them on that basis."[77]

What I draw from this quotation is that within every man there is a measure of light. There is a revelation of knowing right from wrong. All men will be judged by the revelation of light they have in their lives. That includes the saved and the unsaved. But here is the difference the scripture drives home. We, who are no longer Gentiles (sinners), are going to be held to a greater level of judgment because the light in us is greater. See, Paul asks some probing questions: "Do you who teach, teach yourself? Do you who preach against stealing, do you steal? Do you who say that people should not commit adultery, do you commit adultery?" He is asking those who proclaim the truth, are you seeking to live out the truth you preach?

In 2 Timothy 3:16-17 he says, "All scripture is God-breathed and is useful for teaching, rebuking, correcting and training in righteousness, so that the man of God may be thoroughly equipped for every good work."[78] When you put these passages together, we come up with this gripping reality: the word of God was not written and given to us so that we might develop some form of deep theology that sounds impressive. The Bible is the word of God who spoke to men and told them to put pen to paper. The words declared therein are to be the rule and guide for all Christian conduct. Therefore, we cannot pick which parts we like and live only by them. We must also seek to live by the parts with which we may not agree.

Jesus promised in John 16:13, "But when He, the Spirit of Truth comes, He will guide you into all truth."[79] The Holy Spirit will help us to not only understand, He will guide us into all truth. The

Message Bible says, "He will take you by the hand and guide you into all the truth there is."[80] What that tells us is that there is no excuse for Christians to partake in racism. And though some have tried to twist scripture to support their position for separation of the races, there are not scriptures to support them. In fact, 1 John 2:7-11 does exactly the opposite. Here is what it says:

> "Dear friends, I am not writing you a new command but an old one, which you had from the beginning. This old command is the message you have heard. Yet, I am writing you a new command; its truth is seen in Him and you, because the darkness is passing and the true light is already shining. Anyone who claims to be in the light but hates his brother is still in the darkness. Whoever loves his brother lives in the light, and there is nothing in him to make him stumble. But whoever hates his brother is in the darkness and walks around in the darkness; he does not know where he is going because the darkness has blinded him."[81]

These verses of scripture are very important because many times they are used in a very generic way. Pastors use these words from the pulpit implying that the only implication of this scripture is from Christian to Christian. But it runs deeper than that. It means from Christian to Christian, even if the color of that Christians skin differs from mine. John says that the command he is giving us is not something new, but an old command. In fact, he says it was, "from the beginning." The "beginning" in 1 John is the incarnation of Christ. It began with His birth, and it grew into adulthood as He labored as a carpenter and ultimately being fulfilled when He walked through three years of earthly public ministry. He showed the commandment to His disciples and He gave the commandment to His disciples. There are several examples in scripture where Jesus told His disciples that it was about more than preaching about love and talking about love. He told them that love is not a noun, but rather a verb. Love is not reserved for only certain kinds of people, but for all people. In John 15:10-12 we find these words of Jesus:

> *"If you obey my commands, you will remain in my love, just as I have obeyed the father's commands and remain in His love. I have told you this so that my joy may be in you and that your joy may be complete. My commandment is this; love each other as I have loved you."*[82]

Jesus gives this directive: "Love each other as I have loved you." When we love each other as He has loved us, He tells us our joy will be full. In John 13:34-35 He says:

> *"My children, I will be with you only a little while longer. You will look for me, and just as I told the Jews, so will I tell you now: where I am going you cannot come. A new command I give you: love one another. As I have loved you, so must you love one another. By this all men will know that you are my disciples, if you love one another."*[83]

This is the same Jesus who went and asked the Samaritan woman for water. I remind you that there was no love lost between the Samaritans and the Jews. She is the woman to whom Jesus made the declaration that there would come a day when a person's nationality would not inhibit them from worshipping together. This Jesus also then gives us a new commandment to love one another, as He has loved us. Then, John comes along in 1 John 2 and tells us that he is writing to us, not about a new command, but about an old command. He was bringing back to our attention what Jesus already had told us to do: love one another as I have loved you.

LOVE ONE ANOTHER AS I HAVE LOVED YOU.

Then he follows up the statement concerning the old command with the addition of a "new command." The new command is found in verse 8, "Yet I am writing you a new command; its truth is seen in Him and you, because the darkness is passing and the true light is already shining."[84] What we see is that this is a new command, because once we are born again it is no longer simply head knowledge. It is no longer simply words we have heard preached and taught. Now the command becomes something we not only say, it becomes what we do.

Jesus said this is the only identifying marker of our proof that we are His disciples, that we love one another, that we love other Christians. Our Christianity is meant to cause us to love all people, sinners and saints alike. But, Jesus reminds us that we will never show love to the sinner until we have shown the God kind of love to fellow Christians. So John says, "I'm not telling you something new when I tell you to love one another. Jesus told you so." He is trying to reinforce that this revelation came when Jesus was with man on earth. The power to fulfill it by living it out has come now that Jesus has gone back to the Father, and the Holy Spirit has been given to us to lead and guide us into all truth.

In verse 9 John says, "He that saith he is in the light, and hateth his brother, is in darkness even until now."[85] Notice what he says: it is impossible for you to truly walk in the power of confession of

184 | RACISM and the CHURCH

your faith if you hate a fellow Christian. Now, it should go without saying that there are some Christians that it takes a little more power to love than others. Nevertheless, we are called as Jesus' disciples to love even those whom we find to be unlovely.

I heard Dr. J. Vernon McGee tell of the time when he was attending seminary. He roomed with a young man who had, in his estimation, some of the nastiest habits he had ever seen in a Christian. His roommate would start singing at night after Dr. McGee went to bed and was asleep. He wouldn't sing all day, but at eleven o'clock at night he was ready for his routine. Dr. McGee said, "He had a lot of mean habits like that." So one day he told him, "You know, you are the greatest proof to me that I am a child of God."

The roommate asked, "What do you mean?"

Dr. McGee replied, "You are the most nauseating, the most sickening Christian that I have ever met, but I want you to know something, I love you."

His roommate looked right at him and said, "I want you to know that you are the most abominable Christian I have ever met, and I also want you to know that you are the hardest person in the world to love, but I love you."

Years later, Dr. McGee found out that this man got into some trouble. He made the trip to see him, to see if there was anything he could do to help him. He said, "When I met him, I found that he wasn't any more loveable than he had been when I roomed with him. He was even more objectionable, and I think he found me the same, but I didn't hate him. That man was a child of God and God used him mightily in the ministry. In many ways he was a great fellow. I don't know why it is that when a Christian finds he doesn't like somebody, he thinks the alternative is to hate him. You don't have to hate him at all; you are to love him as a child of God."

We must let this be driven into our spirits. When you have a deep seeded hatred of someone, you are in the darkness, and not in the light. If we are truly walking in the light, it must eventually move the darkness from areas where there is no light. The reality is that many times this scripture is preached in partiality and compromise. Preachers declare this truth, instructing parishioners to love one another, as Christ has loved us. Some even boldly proclaim that if there is hatred in one's heart toward another Christian, they are walking in darkness. I have heard some preachers who were bold enough to say that one's salvation is in question if they have hatred in their heart toward another Christian. Yet, many of those same preachers back away when it comes to proclaiming that this scripture applies to all Christian relationships, no matter the ethnicity and color of one's skin. John says, if you hate your brother for any reason, you are in the darkness and not in the light.

Here is the usual argument that people make: "I don't hate people of another race; I just believe they should stay with their own kind." Some struggle because John uses the word hate and that word is so strong that people with racist mentalities feel justified in their thinking because it seems to them to be okay, as long as they don't "hate" someone of a different ethnicity. But, here is what we don't want to miss. John is charging that the very essence of Christianity is love. But, it's not just any kind of love. It's agape love, the God kind of love—the kind of love to which there are no strings attached. It's the kind of love that is not based upon conditions or the meeting of certain criteria. The word of God is clear on this position. The Bible says that anyone who hates his brother is still in the dark. God does not leave any wiggle room in this area. If we are going to break the spirit of racism in the Body of Christ, preachers and parishioners alike must understand there must be a commitment to the integrity of God's Word.

ENDNOTES

1. *The Message (Numbered Edition)*. Ed. Eugene H. Peterson. Colorado Springs, Colorado: Navpress, 2005. Print..

2. *NIV Study Bible (Red Letter Edition)*. Edited by Kenneth Barker. Grand Rapids, Michigan: The Zondervan Corporation, 1985. Print.

3. Ibid.

4. *The Hebrew-Greek Key Study Bible (King James Version)*. Edited By Spiros Zodhiates, Th.D. Chattanooga, Tennessee: AMG Publishers, 1984, 1991. Print.

5. Ibid.

6. Ibid.

7. "The Law of Instrument." Wikipedia. Web. 13 June 2013.

8. *The Hebrew-Greek Key Study Bible (King James Version)*. Edited By Spiros Zodhiates, Th.D. Chattanooga, Tennessee: AMG Publishers, 1984, 1991. Print.

9. Ibid.

10. Ibid.

11. *NIV Study Bible (Red Letter Edition)*. Edited by Kenneth Barker. Grand Rapids, Michigan: The Zondervan Corporation, 1985. Print.

12. Ibid.

13. Ibid.

14. Ibid.

15. Ibid.

16. Ibid.

17. Ibid.

18. *The Message (Numbered Edition)*. Ed. Eugene H. Peterson. Colorado Springs, Colorado: Navpress, 2005. Print.

19. Ibid.

20. Ibid.

21. Britten, Terry. "What's Love Got to Do with It." Tina Turner: Private Dancer 1984. Web. Date Accessed.

22. *NIV Study Bible (Red Letter Edition)*. Edited by Kenneth Barker. Grand Rapids, Michigan: The Zondervan Corporation, 1985. Print.

23. "Great Commission Statistics." Joshua Project. Web. 13 June 2013.

24. *NIV Study Bible (Red Letter Edition).* Edited by Kenneth Barker. Grand Rapids, Michigan: The Zondervan Corporation, 1985. Print.

25. Ibid.

26. Ibid.

27. Ibid.

28. Ibid.

29. Ibid.

30. Ibid.

31. Lucado, Max. *In the Grip of Grace.* Life Aboard the Fellowship: Chapter 16." 4 October 1996. Web. 13 June 2013.

32. *The Hebrew-Greek Key Study Bible (King James Version).* Edited By Spiros Zodhiates, Th.D. Chattanooga, Tennessee: AMG Publishers, 1984, 1991. Print.

33. Ibid.

34. "An Open Book: Ancient Greek conceptions of Love." Close Enough to Read. 3 February 2012. Web. 11 June 2013.

35. Ibid.

36. *The Hebrew-Greek Key Study Bible (King James Version).* Edited By Spiros Zodhiates, Th.D. Chattanooga, Tennessee: AMG Publishers, 1984, 1991. Print..

37. *NIV Study Bible (Red Letter Edition).* Edited by Kenneth Barker. Grand Rapids, Michigan: The Zondervan Corporation, 1985. Print.

38. *The Hebrew-Greek Key Study Bible (King James Version).* Edited By Spiros Zodhiates, Th.D. Chattanooga, Tennessee: AMG Publishers, 1984, 1991. Print.

39. *NIV Study Bible (Red Letter Edition).* Edited by Kenneth Barker. Grand Rapids, Michigan: The Zondervan Corporation, 1985. Print.

40. Ibid.

41. Ibid.

42. Ibid.

43. Ibid.

44. Ibid.

45. Ibid.

46. Ibid.

47. *The American Heritage Dictionary. Second Edition.* Boston, Massachusetts: Houghton Mifflin Company, 1982, 1985. Print.

48. Schoetz, David. "Olympic Team's 'Slant Eyes' Ad Draws Ire." ABC News. 11 February 2009. Web. 18 October 2012.

49. *The American Heritage Dictionary. Second Edition.* Boston, Massachusetts: Houghton Mifflin Company, 1982, 1985. Print.

50. *Microsoft Encarta College Dictionary.* New York, New York: Bloombury Publishing Plc, 2001.

51. *The Message (Numbered Edition).* Ed. Eugene H. Peterson. Colorado Springs, Colorado: Navpress, 2005. Print.

52. *NIV Study Bible (Red Letter Edition).* Edited by Kenneth Barker. Grand Rapids, Michigan: The Zondervan Corporation, 1985. Print.

53. *The Message (Numbered Edition)*. Ed. Eugene H. Peterson. Colorado Springs, Colorado: Navpress, 2005. Print.
54. Edited by Carson, Clayborne. *The Autobiography of Martin Luther King, Jr.* New York, New York: Grand Central Publishing, 1980
55. *NIV Study Bible (Red Letter Edition)*. Edited by Kenneth Barker. Grand Rapids, Michigan: The Zondervan Corporation, 1985. Print.
56. *The Message (Numbered Edition)*. Ed. Eugene H. Peterson. Colorado Springs, Colorado: Navpress, 2005. Print.
57. *NIV Study Bible (Red Letter Edition)*. Edited by Kenneth Barker. Grand Rapids, Michigan: The Zondervan Corporation, 1985. Print.
58. *The Message (Numbered Edition)*. Ed. Eugene H. Peterson. Colorado Springs, Colorado: Navpress, 2005. Print.
59. Ibid.
60. Ibid.
61. Ibid.
62. *Genetics.* The Smithsonian Institution Human Origins Program. Date Posted. Web. 13 June 2013.
63. *NIV Study Bible (Red Letter Edition)*. Edited by Kenneth Barker. Grand Rapids, Michigan: The Zondervan Corporation, 1985. Print.
64. Ibid.
65. NIV Study Bible (Red Letter Edition). Edited by Kenneth Barker. Grand Rapids, Michigan: The Zondervan Corporation, 1985. Print
66. *New American Standard Bible.* Nashville, Tennessee: Holman Bible Publishers, 1981.
67. Edited by Kent Span and David Wheeler. *Nelson's Annual Preacher's Sourcebook – Volume 1.* Nashville Tennessee: Thomas Nelson, Inc., 2011.
68. *NIV Study Bible (Red Letter Edition)*. Edited by Kenneth Barker. Grand Rapids, Michigan: The Zondervan Corporation, 1985. Print.
69. Ibid.
70. Ibid.
71. Ibid.
72. Ibid.
73. Ibid.
74. Ibid.
75. *The Maxwell Leadership Bible (New King James Version)*. Nashville, Tennessee: Thomas Nelson Bibles, 2002.
76. *NIV Study Bible (Red Letter Edition)*. Edited by Kenneth Barker. Grand Rapids, Michigan: The Zondervan Corporation, 1985. Print.
77. McGee, J. Vernon. *Through the Bible with J. Vernon McGee (Volume IV Matthew - Romans).* Nashville, Tennessee: Thomas Nelson Publishers, 1983.
78. *NIV Study Bible (Red Letter Edition)*. Edited by Kenneth Barker. Grand Rapids, Michigan: The Zondervan Corporation, 1985. Print.
79. Ibid.
80. *The Message (Numbered Edition)*. Ed. Eugene H. Peterson. Colorado Springs, Colorado: Navpress, 2005. Print.

81. *NIV Study Bible (Red Letter Edition)*. Edited by Kenneth Barker. Grand Rapids, Michigan: The Zondervan Corporation, 1985. Print.
82. Ibid.
83. Ibid.
84. Ibid.
85. *The Hebrew-Greek Key Study Bible (King James Version)*. Edited By Spiros Zodhiates, Th.D. Chattanooga, Tennessee: AMG Publishers, 1984, 1991. Print.

**IF WE ARE TRULY WALKING IN
THE LIGHT, IT MUST EVENTUALLY
MOVE THE DARKNESS FROM AREAS
WHERE THERE IS NO LIGHT.**

OUR RESPONSIBILITY FOR RACISM IN THE CHURCH

AM I MY BROTHER'S KEEPER?

After Cain had murdered his brother Abel, and God questioned him concerning his brother's whereabouts, with all the power of pride and arrogance, Cain turned and asked God a question instead of answering God (Genesis 4:1-10). Cain responded, "Am I my brother's keeper?" (v. 9).[1] The answer to the question is the same that will cause us to love each other the way we should. If Cain had understood that indeed he was his brother's keeper, he would never have struck that deadly blow and killed him. He would have covered him and protected him because of his love for him.

The Bible declares we are all brothers and sisters in Christ. When we come out of the kingdom of darkness and into the kingdom of light, we become our brother's keeper. Little did Cain understand and little does man today seem to understand that God holds us accountable for our fellow man, and particularly those who are in the kingdom of God. We have not only been saved "from" something, but we have also been saved "unto" something. We have been saved that we might serve God. We serve God by serving our fellow man. The moment we are born again, we become our brother's keeper. We are to become a servant to our fellow man.

Galatians 6:10 says, "Therefore, as we have opportunity, let us do good to all people, especially to those who belong to the family of believers."[2] That scripture instructs Christians to do good to "all" people—even more so when it comes to those who belong to the family of believers. That means the whole family of believers, no matter the color of their skin. The way to do good to all who belong to the family of believers is to allow the Holy Spirit to work in us until we have the heart of a servant. The heart of a true servant of Christ will see every person as one they are responsible for.

In Matthew 20, the mother of Jesus' disciples James and John comes to Jesus with a special seating request. It reminds me of the political games people play in the church where a person being seated in a certain place makes them feel important. Jesus' response to her is that she really does not understand the impact of what would happen, nor the responsibility her sons would carry if He were able to grant her request. He says (v. 22), "You don't know what you are asking." Then He asked them this question, "Can you drink the cup I'm going to drink?" And of course they responded, "We can."[3]

"Jesus said to them, 'You will indeed drink from my cup, but to sit at my right or left is not for me to grant. These places belong to those for who they have been prepared by my father'" (v. 23).[4] Those verses tell us something about the condition of not only James' and John's hearts, but their mother's heart as well. Verse 24 is a revelation of the other disciples' hearts. That verse says that when the other disciples heard the conversation between Jesus and the mother of James and John, they were beside themselves— "They were indignant."[5] The word "indignant" is important because it means they were aroused by something they deemed to be unjust.[6] In their finite minds they could not believe that these two thought so much of themselves that they not only thought they deserved the best seats in the kingdom, but they had the nerve to put their mother up to the dirty work. We don't know if Jesus heard them complaining to one another or if He read their hearts. But when He realized what was going on, He dealt with it (v. 25):

> *"You know that the rulers of the Gentiles lord it over them, and their high officials exercise authority over them. Not so with you. Instead, whoever wants to become great among you must be your servant, and whoever wants to be first must be your slave – just as the Son of Man did not come to be served, but to serve, and to give his life as a ransom for many."*[7]

Deep inside every person there is this desire to be great. It's the flesh man of the three part man that we all are. In all of us, there is this need to feel that we are somebody. The problem is that when it is only flesh, we press others down in order to be lifted up. Jesus told His disciples that if they wanted to be great in the kingdom of God, the way to do it is serve your fellow man.

There is something at the very heart of racism that gives some the need to somehow raise their race above someone of another race. One of the ways Jesus helps us to overcome that need is to become a servant to all people. In Philippians 2:3, Paul gives this instruction, "Let nothing be done through strife or vainglory; but in lowliness of mind let each esteem other better than themselves."[8]

Not only are we to serve one another, but as a Christian, each of us has an obligation to build up the Body of Christ.

I find it hard to believe that someone can truly love God and not be willing to be his brother's keeper. And because we are our brother's keeper, we have an obligation to love all the brethren. In order to really be a servant of all, our love must become more vulnerable. In Matthew 24:14, Jesus said, "Because of the increase of wickedness the love of most people will grow cold."[9] The question we want to answer is, "Is our love growing hotter or colder for the things and the people of God?"

I once heard Francis Frangipane ask these probing questions in a message:

> "Is your love growing and becoming softer and brighter, more daring, and more visible? Or is it becoming more discriminating, more calculating, less vulnerable, and less available? This is a very important issue, for your Christianity is only as real as your love is. A measurable decrease in your ability to love is evidence that the stronghold of cold love is developing within you. A major area of spiritual warfare that has come against the church is in the sphere of church relationships."

Luke 11:17 records these words of Jesus, "But knowing their thoughts Jesus said to them, 'Every kingdom that is divided against itself will be ruined. And a house divided against itself will fall.'"[10] I am convinced that in these last days of the church we will not win the lost because of our big buildings, big programs, and big budgets. We will win them by the one thing that the church lacks most—a commitment to love each other in spite of our differences. We have come to the place where true Christian love must be the order of the day. That true Christian love is lived out through servanthood. Servanthood is born out of the overflow of hot Christian love. When love is cold it shuts down the avenues through which the anointing of the Spirit of God can truly flow. When there is no free flow of the Spirit, we lack the power we need to reach a lost and dying world. Let's look at Titus 3:3-11:

> "At one time we too were foolish, disobedient, deceived and enslaved by all kinds of passions and pleasures. We lived in malice and envy, being hated and hating one another. But when the kindness and love of God our Savior appeared, He saved us, not because of righteous things we had done, but because of His mercy. He saved us through the washing and rebirth and renewal by the Spirit, whom He poured out on to us generously through Jesus Christ our Savior, so that, having been justified by His grace, we might become heirs having the hope of eternal life.

> "This is a trustworthy saying. And I want you to stress these things, so that those who have trusted God may be careful to devote themselves to doing what is good. These things are excellent and profitable for everyone. But avoid foolish controversies and genealogies and arguments and quarrels about the law, because these are unprofitable and useless. Warn a divisive person once, then warn him a second time. After that, have nothing to do with him. You may be sure that such a man is warped and sinful; he is self-condemned."[11]

Those passages of scripture are interesting to me in that many times we apply them to every other sin except this area of racism. Preachers preach against lying, backbiting, malice, bitterness, envy, gossip and many other sins which divide the Body of Christ. But, very few take a bold stance against the sin of racism that divides the body as much, if not more so than any of the other sins.

Verse 3 says that at one time, "We were foolish, disobedient and enslaved to all kinds of passions and pleasures."[12] That verse tells us that "pre-Christ" we operated in and tolerated malice, envy, being hated and hating. Then verse 4 tells us why we should have a change of heart accompanied by a change in actions. Paul says, "But when the kindness and the love of God our Savior appeared, He saved us, not because of righteous things we had done, but because of His mercy."[13] He continues to talk about the blessings God gave us through Jesus Christ our Savior. In verse 8 He says, "And I want you to stress these things, so that those who have trusted in God may be careful to devote themselves to doing what is good."[14]

Paul is telling us that if we truly believe and accept all that God has done for us through Christ Jesus, then there should be a great change in the way we think and behave. We should no longer be dominated by the things He mentioned earlier. We should no longer be dominated by foolishness, disobedience and enslaved to all kinds of passions and pleasures. We should no longer be dominated by spirits of malice, envy and hate.

Several years ago Russ Taff, the former lead singer of the Gospel singing group "The Imperials," sang a song entitled "We Will Stand."[15] The message is powerful. At the peak of its popularity this song was sung in churches all over the world, of every denomination, and by multitudes of Christians of every ethnicity. Here are some of the words:

> *"You're my brother, you're my sister, so take me by the hand,*
> *Together we will work until He comes.*
> *There's no foe that can defeat us if we're walking side by side,*
> *As long as there is love we will stand."*

Then another part of the song says:

> *"I don't care about the label you may wear,*
> *If you believe in Jesus you belong with me"*

I remember being in large youth and church rallies where Christians of all ethnicities would lock arms and rock from side to side with tears in their eyes as this song was sung in unity. I also remember many of these same Christians weeks later behaving toward one another as though we had never sang the song. What really stands out to me is that in many churches where it was evident (and still to this day), that people of a different ethnicity are not welcome, they too sang this song. I fear that in many church arenas we missed the message. In many arenas we were moved by the beauty of the song, rather than the intention it was written for. Russ Taff and the Imperials were trying to drive home the message that, "Yes! I am my brother's keeper!" As long as there is love there is no foe that can defeat us. I am sure there were many who sang that song that really meant and desired to live what they were singing at that moment.

But, what we all must understand, no matter how tolerant we are, is that the only way to truly love our fellow man is to become our brother's keeper. We must come to the place where we sense

198 | **RACISM** and the **CHURCH**

that we do have a responsibility for and toward one another. In fact, the Apostle Paul says this in Romans 13:6-8 concerning the responsibility of our fellowman:

> *"This is also why you pay your taxes, for the authorities are God's servants who give their full time to governing. Give everyone what you owe him: if you owe taxes, pay taxes; if revenue, then revenue; if respect, then respect; if honor, then honor. Let no debt remain outstanding, except the continuing debt to love one another, for he who loves his fellowman has fulfilled the law."[16]*

Most Christians seek to pay their debts off. Though I am sure most Christians are not thrilled on April fifteenth each year, they will pay their taxes. We are to seek to be debt free. Paul says there is one debt that we are never free of: the debt to love our fellow man. This is an ongoing debt as my brother's keeper. The word "love" in this passage is the same word for love used in Galatians 5 concerning the Fruit of the Spirit. It is the Greek word *"agape."* It is a love that has no strings attached and requirements attached to it. Paul says that is the continuing debt or responsibility that I have toward my fellow man, for indeed, I am my brother's keeper.

INDEED, I AM MY BROTHER'S KEEPER.

In Romans 13:9-10 Paul says, "'Do not commit adultery,' 'Do not murder,' 'Do not steal,' 'Do not covet,' and whatever other commandment there may be, are summed up in this one rule: 'Love your neighbor as yourself.' Love does no harm to its neighbor. Therefore love is the fulfillment of the law."[17]

Paul takes love to a whole different level when he asserts that at the end of the day, the key to keeping every commandment is wrapped up in agape love. The ability to live out agape love is found in loving our neighbor as we love ourselves. There is food for thought. If indeed my love for myself is healthy, my love for my fellow man will also be healthy, which brings us back to a commitment to biblical love.

This commitment to biblical love must be a work of the Holy Spirit. For none of us is fully capable of loving with the continuing debt of agape love without the help of the Holy Spirit. In Galatians 5:19, Paul says, "the acts of the sinful flesh are obvious."[18] As he lists them, he puts hatred right in the middle of the list. Then in verse 21, he says, "I warn you, as I did before, that those who live like this will not inherit the kingdom of God."[19]

It is time for the Body of Christ to take seriously the command to love one another. That means to love every one of God's children, no matter the color of their skin. Either God's word is not true, or the church needs to repent of those things which we have tolerated and sometimes perpetrated that keep us divided. We must begin to take seriously the responsibility to continually pay the debt of love that we continually owe, whether we accept it or not.

When Paul said, "I warn you, as I did before that those who live like this will not inherit the kingdom ..."[20] he was addressing people who felt that because they were saved and under grace, their new found freedom in Christ also freed them to live life as they chose. He was speaking to people who in spite of truth being revealed to them, they desired to keep on living in opposition to God's word.

Then he says to those who desire to truly obey God that there is a power to help you do what you cannot do in your own power. He says in Galatians 5:22, "But the fruit of the spirit is love, joy, peace, patience, goodness, faithfulness and self-control."[21]

The very first fruit is "love." And he says above in verse 25 that the answer to the way to have the fruit of love and the rest of the fruit working continually in our lives is this, "Since we live by the Spirit, let us keep step in step with the Spirit."[22]

In his book, *The Sensitivity of the Spirit,* Dr. R.T. Kendall tells of the time when he was addressing a group of missionaries in the south of France. He was staying in the home of a Christian missionary who at one time had been a Muslim. He was astonished at this change of life and marveled at the missionary's conversion. This missionary told Dr. Kendall that he had been led to Christ by some British soldiers when he lived in Madagascar. But, what Dr. Kendall really wanted to know was what had actually won him to Christianity. Dr. Kendall asked the former Muslim, "What argument did they use? What line of reasoning persuaded you to turn from Islam to the Christian faith?" The missionary responded, "It wasn't what they said. It was who they were!"

That is what the Holy Spirit is meant to perform in the heart of every Christian. He has come to make us attractive to the world so that they might look at us and see something that causes us to have favor with all men. He has come to cause us to become love and not just talk love. If there is something that the church needs to realize and desire it is to be possessed and consumed by the Holy Spirit of God.

There is something that has been missed in a lot of churches when it comes to the Holy Spirit. While the fruit of the spirit is produced by the inner working of the supernatural power of God in us, there must also be a corresponding desire and response of obedience by God's children. The Holy Spirit is the third person of the Trinity which means that He has the personality or character traits inherent in the Holy Spirit of which He is a gentleman. Thus, while He will inform us of God's desires, He will not force God's desire upon us. But, if we submit our will in cooperation with the Holy Spirit, He then will produce the fruit of the Spirit in our lives. That means that while the Spirit will work through me, I must give Him room to work by making the decision to take responsibility to be my brother's keeper. The way I do that is to determine to love my neighbor as myself. When we do that, then the Holy Spirit comes along and empowers us to do what we have committed to do.

Whenever we desire to please and obey the Father, there is always a two-fold work going on in our lives. It is the Holy Spirit working in me because He has come to aid me, and the Holy Spirit working through me because I have submitted my will to the will of the Father. For the church of Jesus Christ to become truly committed to dealing with racism in the church, there must also be a submission of our wills to the will of the Father. I have seen the bumper stickers … and I grew up hearing the words sung about the bumper sticker that says, "Be patient with me. God's not through with me yet." I thank God that He's not through with any of us, yet. But, it does not negate our responsibility to seek to obey God in every way.

In the Body of Christ there are those who believe that love is some kind of emotion. That love is some kind of feeling. And therefore, many believe that love is uncontrollable, which in turns means that loving my fellowman is something that has to happen over the course of time as the Holy Spirit works on them. That is only partially true. Love is something we can control. Love is something that we have a responsibility for.

WHAT THE BIBLE SAYS ABOUT LOVE

While Galatians tells us that love is a fruit of the spirit, the word of God also defines love as something we do alongside the Holy Spirit. Here are some of the things the Bible says about man's part when it comes to love:

- **WE CHOOSE TO LOVE OR NOT TO LOVE.**

  Colossians 3:14 says, "And over all virtues, put on love, which binds them all together in perfect unity."[23] The word of God does not say "feel" love. Colossians says that we are to "put on love." It is like a cloak that we can take off and put on. That means that it is my choice to love in any and every situation and circumstance. I have heard people make this unbelievable statement, "Love is an uncontrollable reflex." I say, "No! Love is a choice."

- **LOVE IS A MATTER OF BEHAVIOR.**

  I John 3:18 says, "Dear children, let us not love with words or tongue but with actions and truth."[24] John tells us to back up our talk with our walk. To back up what we say with what we do. I heard the story of a young man who was always saying to his girlfriend, "Oh, honey, I would die for you." One day she said to him, "Oh, you're always telling me that, but you never do it." She was talking about sacrificial love. That young man's girl was saying, "Talk is cheap but harder to keep." Though she was joking, there is an element of truth to her statement. She was saying that real love is accompanied by corresponding behavior. It's interesting that in the church of Jesus Christ, we so often talk about sacrificial love, but never get around to it. To break the spirit of racism, as we talked about earlier will take sacrificial love.

For the church to raise a standard against the spirit of racism, we must raise our standard and requirement of love. 2 Corinthians 3:2-3 is the gut reality when it comes to the Body of Christ and what we decide to do with this issue of racism. Paul writes this to the church of Corinth:

"You, yourselves are our letter, written on our hearts, known and read by everybody. You show that you are a letter from Christ, the result of our ministry, written not with ink but with the Spirit of the Living God, not on tablets of stone but on tablets of human hearts."[25]

When I read those verses, they remind me of a truth I have witnessed over and over in my few short years on earth: people will remember what we do long after they have forgotten what we have said. Satan works overtime seeking to keep the church of Jesus Christ divided, dysfunctional and delayed from our destiny through the spirit of racism because he knows that if we break this barrier, the anointing to set men free will flow without restraint.

Let me close with this true account of how God can break the power of the spirit of racism if we will submit to His Holy Spirit. Back in the mid-90s I was serving as the youth pastor for First Assembly of God in Worcester, Massachusetts. During that time it was a big deal to do teachings on rock music. As I began a series, word got out in the community that I was teaching on Thursday nights in youth group "The Truth Concerning Rock Music." A mother who was a Jehovah's Witness brought her son and daughter to my seminars. Her son was into heavy metal music. He even had the long hair and earrings to match the music. In the process of bringing them, not only did the kids get saved, but so did the mother. They started coming to church on Sunday mornings and Sunday nights as they continued to attend youth group. This did not sit well with her anti-Christian, millionaire husband.

One Thursday night she came to me to inform me that they could continue to come on Thursday nights but not on Sunday mornings because her husband decided he wanted her on the yacht with him on Sundays. So she made him a deal. She agreed to be with him on Sundays if he could come to church with her on Thursday evenings. He reluctantly and angrily agreed. She started bringing him to youth group on Thursday nights.

The first night as my wife and I were milling around among the youth, this woman and her children walked in, angry husband in tow. I immediately set out to greet him. She rushed up to me before I could get near him and announced to me, "Don't say anything to my husband. He hates black people and said if you said anything to him, he would kill you." She then told me the source of his hatred. His sister was married to his former best friend who was a black man. This friend murdered his sister.

From that day forward he had made up his mind to hate all black people and never trust them again.

That night he sat through the whole youth service with this angry look. Immediately after the service was over, he rushed his family out of the building. My heart was so grieved I asked the Lord what to do. The Holy Spirit spoke to me that each service I should face the piano in his direction and as I led worship to pray for him in the Spirit. For several weeks I simply obeyed the Holy Spirit. Then it happened one night in youth group. No, he did not try to kill me! But in the middle of the worship I felt the Spirit instruct me to give an altar call for salvation. Before I could finish giving the invitation, young people started jumping out of their seats and moving toward the altar. That within itself was powerful. But what was even more powerful was that they were being led by this woman's husband. He had jumped out of his seat and ran so fast toward the altar that he tripped and fell and slid, bumping his face on the edge of the platform.

That night, he wept his way to Jesus and he and I became best friends. God took our relationship and opened a door for me, him, and another friend to go into prisons and public high schools and minister to youth in the Worcester area. God not only broke the racial barrier that separated man from man, but he used us to begin breaking racial barriers in the schools and the community as a whole.

I am so thankful to the Lord for breaking down that wall, because within a few short months of saving my friend, he died in a boating accident. What has stayed with me was when I asked him what the turning point was for him, he told me that in spite of how mean he was to me, I continued to just look at him and smile. He said, "You didn't just preach love, you showed it."

THE CONCLUSION OF THE MATTER

"You yourselves are our letter, written on our hearts, known and read by everybody. You show that you are a letter from Christ, the result of our ministry, written not with ink but with the Spirit of the Living God, not on tablet of stone but on tablets of human hearts."

—2 Corinthians 3:2-3

"They devoted themselves to the apostles teaching and to the fellowship, to the breaking of bread and to prayer. Everyone was filled with awe, and many wonders and miraculous signs were done by the apostles. All the believers were together and had everything in common. Selling their possessions and goods, they gave to anyone in need. Every day they continued to meet together in the temple courts. They broke bread in their homes and ate together with glad and sincere hearts, praising God and enjoying the favor of all the people. And the Lord added to their number daily those who were being saved."

—Acts 2:42-47

Amen and amen!

E N D N O T E S

1. *The Hebrew-Greek Key Study Bible (King James Version)*. Edited By Spiros Zodhiates, Th.D. Chattanooga, Tennessee: AMG Publishers, 1984, 1991. Print.
2. *NIV Study Bible (Red Letter Edition)*. Edited by Kenneth Barker. Grand Rapids, Michigan: The Zondervan Corporation, 1985. Print.
3. Ibid.
4. Ibid.
5. Ibid.
6. *The American Heritage Dictionary. Second Edition*. Boston, Massachusetts: Houghton Mifflin Company, 1982, 1985. Print.
7. *NIV Study Bible (Red Letter Edition)*. Edited by Kenneth Barker. Grand Rapids, Michigan: The Zondervan Corporation, 1985. Print.
8. *The Hebrew-Greek Key Study Bible (King James Version)*. Edited By Spiros Zodhiates, Th.D. Chattanooga, Tennessee: AMG Publishers, 1984, 1991. Print.
9. *NIV Study Bible (Red Letter Edition)*. Edited by Kenneth Barker. Grand Rapids, Michigan: The Zondervan Corporation, 1985. Print.
10. Ibid.
11. Ibid.
12. Ibid.
13. Ibid.
14. Ibid.
15. Taff, Russ. "We Will Stand." *Russ Taff: Walls of Glass,* 1983. Word Music. Web. 14 June 2013.
16. *NIV Study Bible (Red Letter Edition)*. Edited by Kenneth Barker. Grand Rapids, Michigan: The Zondervan Corporation, 1985. Print.
17. Ibid.
18. Ibid.
19. Ibid.
20. Ibid.
21. Ibid.
22. Ibid.
23. Ibid.
24. Ibid.
25. Ibid.

FOR THE CHURCH TO RAISE A STANDARD AGAINST THE SPIRIT OF RACISM, WE MUST RAISE OUR STANDARD AND REQUIREMENT OF LOVE.

APPENDIX

The following images are to provide you with a visual reference to several of the topics discussed in this thesis with regards to racism in the church and society as a whole. Some will simply identify a key person or event of illustration while others will give a realistic view of the severe consequences of the acts of racism.

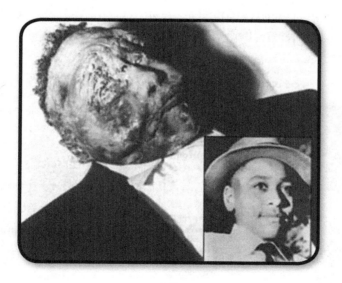

IMAGE 1

Pictures of Emmett Till: the last photo taken of him alive at the age of 14, and the photo of him in his casket at the viewing of the body.

Photo Credit: www.dailyrepublic.com

IMAGE 2

Young Emmett's mother at the arrival of the wooden box
containing her brutally beaten and disfigured son.

Photo Credit: www.dailyrepublic.com

IMAGE 3

Taken in the courtroom of
the Emmet Till case featuring
the cotton gin Emmett's
bludgeoned body was tied to.

Photo Credit: www.dailyrepublic.com

IMAGES 4 AND 5

Trayvon Martin and George Zimmerman.

Photo Credit: www.wikipedia.org

IMAGES 6 AND 7

Civil Rights leaders Dr. Martin Luther King and his son, Dexter Scott King.

Photo Credit Dr. King: www.rolexblog.blogspot.com

Photo Credit Dexter Scott King: heatandanger.files.wordpress.com

IMAGES 8 AND 9

Photos illustrate horrific effects the Holocaust had on European
Jews and minorities by way of concentration camps.

Photo Credit: www.wikipedia.org

IMAGE 10

Adolf Hitler, Germany's leader and the antagonist of WW II, was responsible for the deaths of an estimated 6 million Jews, blacks, gypsies, homosexuals, and physically and mentally disabled human lives.

Photo Credit: www.wikipedia.org

IMAGE 11

"The Fab Five."

Photo Credit: www.wikipedia.org

IMAGE 12

Jimmy "The Greek" Snyder

Photo Credit: www.sportsandcinema.com

IMAGE 13

Dr. Charles Drew

Photo Credit: www.wikipedia.org

IMAGE 14

Spain's Basketball Team making "Chinese eyes" at the 2008 Summer Olympics.

Photo Credit: www.npr.org

IMAGE 15

People dressed in black face in celebration of the
Dutch Christmas tradition of "Black Pete."

Photo Credit: www.thisfragiletent.com

FOR THE CHURCH TO RAISE A STANDARD
AGAINST THE SPIRIT OF RACISM,
WE MUST RAISE OUR STANDARD
AND REQUIREMENT OF LOVE.

DR. JAMES E. COLLINS

James E. Collins, M. Div., Ph.D. serves as senior pastor and visionary of the ethnically and socially diverse Eagle Heights Church in Revere, Massachusetts. He is committed to train this congregation through in-depth biblical, heartfelt preaching and teaching. A dynamic and experienced speaker, Dr. Collins is a true servant-leader with a sincere heart.

This powerful voice of spiritual guidance extends beyond the church to the ears of thousands through "Beyond the Walls" Radio Ministry on WEZE AM590 and WROL AM950 Boston. Dr. Collins has wholly committed his life to reaching the world for Christ, most recently partnering with CCIF (Crossroads Community International Fellowship-Central America) training and developing pastors and leaders in the South American nation of Peru.

He is the founder of the EHC Pastoral Leadership Forum where he serves as a mentor to young pastors and others in church leadership. Dr. Collins teaches them through his own ministry experience, encouraging them to find strength, commitment, stability and security in fulfilling the call to true pastoral leadership. His passion for the Word and desire that more people would adopt a biblical world view has led the charge to open Eagle Heights Bible College in June 2013.

Dr. Collins is joined in ministry with his wife of more than thirty years, Brenda, and his two daughters, Jessica and Shawna.

TO LEARN MORE

visit: www.ehconline.org

TO CONTACT DR. JAMES E. COLLINS

email: drjamesecollinsministries@echonline.org

Made in the USA
Middletown, DE
18 June 2020

98015893R00126